This Book Belongs to...

_____

Imagine Air

COPYRIGHT © 2005 Nanci Bell
Gander Publishing
412 Higuera Street, Suite 200
San Luis Obispo, CA 93401
805-541-5523 • 800-554-1819

VISUALIZING AND VERBALIZING IS A REGISTERED TRADEMARK OF NANCI BELL

ISBN 0-945856-27-X

SEE TIME FLY

Visualizing and Verbalizing® WORKBOOK

VOLUME TWO
1454 to 1610

A Timeline of History for the Renaissance

Nanci Bell

Hey, it's me again. Remember me? I'm Ivan—King of the Neighborhood and king of anything to do with human history. You didn't forget me, did you? Of course not. I'm not sure how I became a professor of human history. It must be that I'm so very fond of you humans.

This workbook is to help you before and after each Flight. You'll get to take a break and read words, learn new vocabulary, check your imagery with comprehension questions for the whole Flight, and write a story! I made it fun! You'll write a long story, not just a line or two, right?

Remember, you can do this. You can do anything...just like me!

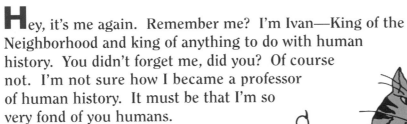

Preread words for each paragraph:

Study and visualize the vocabulary:

1

during	spread	healthy
Middle Ages	Europe	brought
plague	barren	Italy
deadly	tradesmen	appeared
disease	products	education

Date: 8-3

plague: any fast-spreading deadly disease (n.)
barren: having no life; unfertile (adj.)
blacksmith: a worker who makes or fixes things of iron (n.)
merchants: people who buy and sell things for a living (n.)
cargo: goods carried by ship or other means; large supplies of goods (n.)

2

major	businesses	Medici
routes	private	neighbors
Muslim	tutors	building
countries	economy	public
learn	Florence	library

Date: 9

routes: the courses or roads which one takes (n.)
Muslim: of or from the religion of Islam (adj.)
tutors: people who are hired to teach one or more students outside of a classroom (
labor: hard work (n.)
academy: a private school that focuses its teachings on certain subjects (n.)

3

involved	built	painters
throughout	commissioned	sculptors
wealth	works	create
soon	Cosimo	amount
ruled	support	

Date: 9-7

wealth: money or things of value (n.)
commissioned: paid an artist to create something (v.)
support: to give money or provide food and shelter; to give encouragement (v.)
sculptors: people who create art out of stone, ice, clay, etc. by chiseling and scraping (n
surge: a sudden and strong increase (n.)

4

famous	crowds	adored
took	musicians	known
exciting	writers	magnificent
musical	artists	
concerts		

Date: 9-14

concerts: performances where people play before a live audience (n.)
musicians: people who play or write music for a living (n.)
adored: worshiped or loved deeply (v.)
magnificent: full of grace and beauty; wonderful, amazing (adj.)

5

literature	notice	survive
visited	terrible	access
impressed	starvation	blossomed
improve	peasants	Renaissance
touch	poor	world

Date: ____

rebirth: when something is found or done again after a long time (n.)
literature: the written works of a society, often meaning books (n.)
poverty: the state of being without money or possessions; very poor (n.)
peasants: poor people, usually farmers or workers, of low social rank (n.)
Renaissance: a period of time when the arts and education flourished in Europe (n.

Mark this Flight on your timeline:

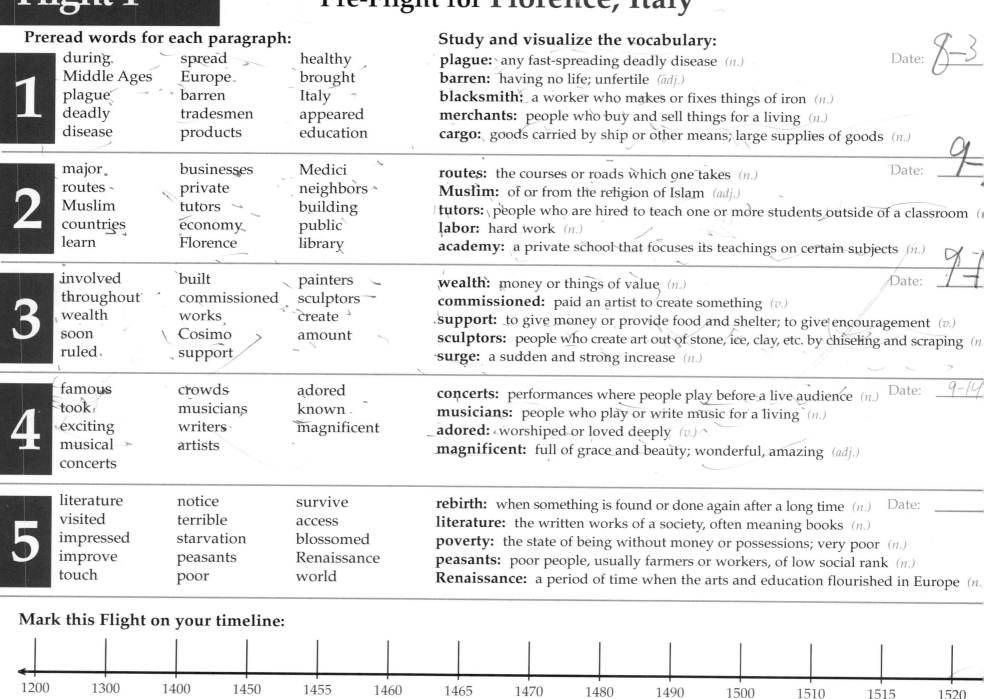

| 1200 | 1300 | 1400 | 1450 | 1455 | 1460 | 1465 | 1470 | 1480 | 1490 | 1500 | 1510 | 1515 | 1520 |

Post-Flight Debriefing

Use your imagery to answer questions for the whole Flight:

A. What is the main idea for this Flight?

_____

_____

_____

B. Which of these things is true about Florence during the 1400's?

    a) The people grew poor and hungry.
    b) The middle class of bankers and merchants disappeared.
    c) It was a trading center for goods from the Far East.
    d) Children had to work in family businesses and had no time to learn.

C. Why do you think the people of Florence became interested in the arts?

    a) Many artists moved there.
    b) They had more money and free time.
    c) Farming was terribly boring.
    d) The plague had killed over a quarter of the population.

D. Why was Florence an important city during the 1400's?

_____

_____

_____

Summarize all you have visualized about Florence, Italy.

_____

_____

_____

_____

_____

_____

_____

_____

_____

_____

_____

_____

_____

530   1535   1540   1545   1550   1555   1565   1575   1585   1600   1700   1800   1900   2000

Flight 2

Pre-Flight for **Humanism**

Preread words for each paragraph:

Study and visualize the vocabulary:

1

humanism	worthy	beautiful
survival	deserved	force
choices	humanistic	idea
improve	thought	
said		

humanism: a way of thinking that embraces the arts and learning *(n.)* Date: _____
choices: things one may pick from; options *(n.)*
created: made; caused to come about *(v.)*
worthy: having value or merit *(adj.)*
idea: a thought, plan, or belief *(n.)*

2

afford	ancient	curiosity
educated	subjects	dangerous
great	science	rebellion
writings	anatomy	praised
scientific	logic	

discovery: when something is found or seen for the first time *(n.)* Date: _____
ancient: from a long time ago *(adj.)*
logic: a way of thinking which helps explain something *(n.)*
curiosity: a desire to learn about new things *(n.)*
rebellion: a fight against the people in power *(n.)*

3

Petrarch	though	poetry
Italian	married	believed
opinionated	expressing	translated
monk	poet laureate	Cicero
Laura		

opinionated: having strong beliefs about things *(adj.)* Date: _____
monk: a man who has devoted his life to religion *(n.)*
expressing: telling or stating *(v.)*
poetry: poems or the writing of poems; words in verse form *(n.)*
translated: changed from one language into another *(v.)*

4

Boccaccio	witty	mythical
popular	describes	knights
medieval	unusual	heroes
romances	real	society
Decameron		

medieval: of or from the Middle Ages *(adj.)* Date: _____
witty: clever and amusing *(adj.)*
realistic: dealing with the facts or the way things are *(adj.)*
identify: to connect with or feel close to someone else *(v.)*
mythical: spoken about in old legends and stories *(adj.)*

5

affected	epidemic	examining
importantly	studying	nature
discoveries	grammar	finding
widespread		

classes: groups of people having different amounts of money and power *(n.)* Date: _____
epidemic: a disease that spreads quickly through a group of people *(n.)*
ethics: codes of moral standards *(n.)*
examining: looking closely at something or testing it *(v.)*

Mark this Flight on your timeline:

← 1200 1300 1400 1450 1455 1460 1465 1470 1480 1490 1500 1510 1515 1520

4

Post-Flight Debriefing

Date: _____

**Flight #2
Humanism**

Use your imagery to answer questions for the whole Flight:

Write a Word Summary for Humanism.

A. What is the main idea for this Flight?

B. Which of these is the best definition for Humanism?

a) a way of thinking that focuses on human values and behavior
b) a theory that says humans should control the buying and selling of goods
c) the study of human anatomy
d) the idea that all humans should have the right to vote

C. Which of these people was a leader of Humanist thought?

b) Petrarch
c) Cicero
d) Socrates

D. Why do you think Humanism became so popular?

530 1535 1540 1545 1550 1555 1565 1575 1585 1600 1700 1800 1900 2000

Pre-Flight for Dante

Preread words for each paragraph:

Study and visualize the vocabulary:

1

prior	divine	character
glorified	nearly	through
beauty	combination	heaven
Dante	values	purgatory
famous	imagery	virtues

epic: grand; heroic *(adj.)*
combination: something made of other things put together *(n.)*
values: beliefs or standards *(n.)*
flaws: defects or imperfections *(n.)*
virtues: good qualities like kindness and generosity *(n.)*

Date: _____

2

position	Beatrice	troubles
politics	sight	desire
Gemma	except	enemies
sweetheart	political	couldn't

position: a job or place of employment *(n.)*
politics: the activities of government leaders *(n.)*
sweetheart: a lover or loved one *(n.)*
political: having to do with politics *(adj.)*
enemies: people who hate and want to hurt others *(n.)*

Date: _____

3

Catholics	forgiveness	whom
soul	journey	symbols
death	ghost	pure
chance	Virgil	whose
repenting	sees	

repenting: feeling sorry about something that's been done *(v.)*
forgiveness: release from guilt or blame *(n.)*
spirits: the souls of people not connected with their bodies *(n.)*
symbols: objects that stand for ideas *(n.)*

Date: _____

4

ages	demons	glory
vivid	blood	imagined
imagery	headless	different
hordes	angels	clouds
bees		

vivid: bright and full of life *(adj.)*
sinners: people who have broken religious rules *(n.)*
suffering: feeling intense pain *(v.)*
hordes: swarms or large crowds *(n.)*
host: an army or large group *(n.)*

Date: _____

5

scary	read	style
stories	imaginations	using
brought	courage	pictures

sparked: stirred up, made active *(v.)*
courage: bravery, confidence *(n.)*
style: a manner of speaking or writing *(n.)*
norm: the standard that other things are judged against *(n.)*

Date: _____

Mark this Flight on your timeline:

1200	1300	1400	1450	1455	1460	1465	1470	1480	1490	1500	1510	1515	1520

Post-Flight Debriefing

Use your imagery to answer questions for the whole Flight:

A. What is the main concept for this Flight?

_____

_____

_____

B. Which of these best describes what Dante's epic poem, *The Divine Comedy*, is about?

  a) angels laughing and rejoicing in Heaven
  b) Dante's personal journey through Heaven, Hell, and Purgatory
  c) a handsome prince named Virgil who falls in love with Beatrice
  d) a scary dream Dante had about Hell, Heaven, and Purgatory

C. Which of these is NOT an image from *The Divine Comedy*?

  a) bats flying overhead while Dante is trapped in a dark cave
  b) scary monsters and demons
  c) a host of angels singing in Heaven
  d) sinners in Hell being stung by bees

D. What made Dante's *Divine Comedy* different from other written works of his time?

_____

Dante and Virgil came out of the cave into the bright light and heat, and all around them were...

_____

_____

_____

_____

_____

_____

_____

_____

_____

_____

_____

_____

_____

| 530 | 1535 | 1540 | 1545 | 1550 | 1555 | 1565 | 1575 | 1585 | 1600 | 1700 | 1800 | 1900 | 2000 |

Flight 4

Pre-Flight for Chaucer

Preread words for each paragraph:

Study and visualize the vocabulary:

1

Geoffrey   normal   energy
Chaucer   putting   humor
considered   inn   drama
greatest   full   English
influenced

Date: _____

considered: thought to be; regarded as *(v.)*
influenced: had an effect on; changed *(v.)*
relate: connect with or feel close to *(v.)*
inn: a hotel; a place for people to eat and sleep in exchange for money *(n.)*
drama: a tense and exciting part of a story *(n.)*

2

Canterbury   ordinary   heroic
travelers   cook   rooster
England   friar   Chanticleer
evenings   wife   crow
weary

Date: _____

pilgrims: people who take a trip to a holy place *(n.)*
weary: tired and worn out *(adj.)*
friar: a type of Catholic monk *(n.)*
shipman: a sailor *(n.)*

3

herbs   appears   escapes
afraid   eager   moral
hear   catch   avoid
compliment   convinces   proud
begins   mouth

Date: _____

herbs: plants that can be used as medicine or to season food *(n.)*
compliment: something said in praise *(n.)*
eager: with great desire; anxious *(adj.)*
moral: the lesson taught *(n.)*
avoid: to keep away from and not take part in *(v.)*

4

quest   lose   pleases
women   shining   magically
answer   armor   disloyal
queen   charge   wrinkled
right   husbands   choose

Date: _____

quest: a journey for a specific purpose *(n.)*
armor: metal plates worn by a knight for protection *(n.)*
in charge: having authority over *(adj.)*
loyal: being true to a person or ideal *(adj.)*

5

extremely   lifetime   Westminster
sought   monument   Abbey
aloud   tomb   honor

Date: _____

extremely: very greatly *(adv.)*
sought: wanted or looked for *(v.)*
monument: a tablet or statue set up to honor someone *(n.)*
tomb: a vault where a dead body is stored *(n.)*

Mark this Flight on your timeline:

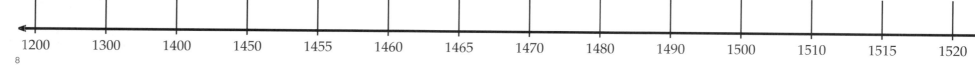

1200   1300   1400   1450   1455   1460   1465   1470   1480   1490   1500   1510   1515   1520

Post-Flight Debriefing

Use your imagery to answer questions for the whole Flight:

A. What is the main idea for this Flight?

_____

_____

_____

B. Who did Chaucer think people would relate to better?

   a) kings
   b) normal people
   c) gods
   d) knights

C. What was the moral of the story about Chanticleer?

   a) A bird in the hand is worth two in the bush.
   b) Don't count your chickens until they've hatched.
   c) Never trust a fox to help you.
   d) Learn from your mistakes.

D. How were Chaucer's stories presented to the public and why?

Write a Picture Summary based on all your images.

530   1535   1540   1545   1550   1555   1565   1575   1585   1600   1700   1800   1900   2000

Flight 5 — Pre-Flight for The Printing Press

Preread words for each paragraph:

Study and visualize the vocabulary:

1

Date: _____

costly, hired, religious, clerics, hours
priests, carefully, drawings, illuminations, whole
thrown, addition, spotted, meant, accurate

costly: having a high price *(adj.)*
clerics: people who wrote and kept records for the Church *(n.)*
illuminations: drawings in the margins of a book's pages *(n.)*
accurate: exact and free from mistakes *(adj.)*

2

Date: _____

copying, Chinese, scrolls, wooden, wears
easily, bronze, Europeans, isolated, civilized
undiscovered, Marco Polo, onward, available, inexpensive

scrolls: rolls of paper with writing on them *(n.)*
carve: to shape by cutting *(v.)*
bronze: a metal made by mixing copper and tin *(n.)*
plates: flat thin pieces of metal *(n.)*
isolated: alone or set apart *(adj.)*

3

Date: _____

Johannes, Gutenberg, German, perfected, movable
tiny, alphabet, poured, molten, lead
sentences, individual, useless, bound, fraction

goldsmith: a craftsman who makes things out of gold *(n.)*
movable: can be moved from one place to another *(adj.)*
mold: a hollow form used to make many things with the same shape *(n.)*
molten: melted by heat *(adj.)*
form: a wooden frame or box built to hold something in place; shape *(n.)*

4

Date: _____

Bible, thousands, taken, quickly, anyone
opinion, notices, doors, daily
latest, record, passed, generations

press: a machine that prints by pressing ink onto the paper *(n.)*
opinion: an idea or belief about something *(n.)*
notices: papers with brief announcements *(n.)*
generations: the different levels of a family, such as parents and children *(n.)*
word of mouth: passed on between people by talking *(n.)*

5

Date: _____

pleased, controlled, scribes
preferred, texts
high, encouraged

scribes: people who copy books and papers by hand *(n.)*
lords: noblemen who ruled lands and people for the king *(n.)*
preferred: to have liked something better *(v.)*
texts: books or copies of a written work *(n.)*
demand: much wanted and looked for *(n.)*

Mark this Flight on your timeline:

1200 1300 1400 1450 1455 1460 1465 1470 1480 1490 1500 1510 1515 1520

10

Post-Flight Debriefing

Use your imagery to answer questions for the whole Flight:

Write a Word Summary for this Flight.

A. How would you summarize this Flight?

_____

_____

_____

B. How were books made in Europe before the printing press?

    a) They were written and copied by hand.
    b) They were printed using wooden blocks and paint.
    c) They were made on a computer.
    d) They were made by carving stone blocks.

C. What did Gutenberg do to perfect the method of printing?

    a) He developed special inks in bright colors.
    b) He invented a method for engraving on gold.
    c) He developed a process using water and sand.
    d) He invented movable metal type and the wooden form.

D. What did Gutenberg print first, and why?

_____

_____

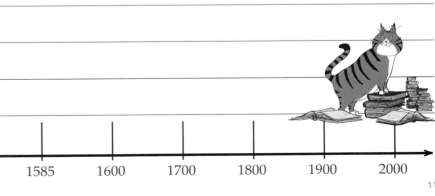

530   1535   1540   1545   1550   1555   1565   1575   1585   1600   1700   1800   1900   2000

1

Preread words for each paragraph:

Allessandro	Botticelli	moment
Filipepi	barrel	immersed
Sandro	study	developing
precision	Filippo Lippi	natural
design	changing	humanity

Study and visualize the vocabulary:

Date: _____

sickly: weak and poor in health *(adj.)*
precision: the quality of being accurate and exact *(n.)*
keg: a small barrel or container made of wood *(n.)*
immersed: jumped into and absorbed, as with water *(v.)*
humanity: all people *(n.)*

2

nobles	portraits	heavily
delicate	studio	court
attention	trying	among
supporting	balance	practical
series	naturalist	students

Date: _____

nobles: people who have wealth and a high position in society *(n.)*
delicate: looking beautifully light and fine *(adj.)*
series: a group of similar things, one after another *(n.)*
portraits: paintings of people or a person *(n.)*
naturalist: showing plants and animals true to reality *(adj.)*

3

struggling	chapel	Christ
invited	chose	beloved
murals	trials	refusing
frescoes	Moses	due
Sistine	temptation	problems

Date: _____

murals: large pictures painted onto walls *(n.)*
frescoes: paintings done with watercolors on wet plaster *(n.)*
temptation: the act of trying to get someone to do something they shouldn't *(n.)*
refusing: turning down; not accepting *(v.)*
due: because of or owing to *(conj.)*

4

several	example	almost
career	unique	giant
earning	figure	awe
mythology	goddess	transparent
ethereal	Venus	ghostly

Date: _____

peak: the highest or greatest part *(n.)*
ethereal: light, airy, and delicate; ghostly *(adj.)*
unique: the only one of its kind *(adj.)*
transparent: see through; clear like glass *(adj.)*
divinely: as a god or goddess *(adv.)*

5

Savonarola	allowed	earlier
hook	scenes	penniless
eyes	already	kindness
enforced	zeal	continued
strict		

Date: _____

beady: small and round like a pebble or bead *(adj.)*
enforced: required and carried out by force *(v.)*
strict: enforcing the rules very closely *(adj.)*
zeal: strong enthusiasm or excitement *(n.)*
penniless: having no money at all *(adj.)*

Mark this Flight on your timeline:

1200 1300 1400 1450 1455 1460 1465 1470 1480 1490 1500 1510 1515 1520

Post-Flight Debriefing

Use your imagery to answer questions for the whole Flight:

Write a Word Summary for Botticelli.

A. What is the main concept for this Flight?

_____

_____

_____

B. What did Botticelli learn from working for a goldsmith?

a) Gold was a soft metal, easily pounded into different shapes.
b) precision and how to draw clean lines
c) how to draw human anatomy properly
d) the right way to wind a watch

C. What style was Botticelli known for in his paintings?

a) He painted scenes of battle and war with realism.
b) He painted portraits of the kings and queens, making them prettier.
c) He painted animals into all of his paintings in an abstract style.
d) He painted mythological scenes in a soft, ghostly style.

D. Why might Botticelli have felt he needed to burn his own paintings?

_____

_____

_____

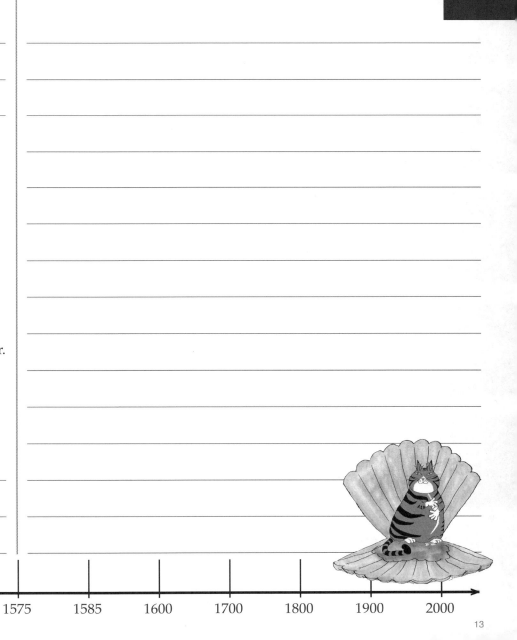

530   1535   1540   1545   1550   1555   1565   1575   1585   1600   1700   1800   1900   2000

Pre-Flight for Isabella of Spain

Preread words for each paragraph:

Study and visualize the vocabulary:

1

strongest	castle	fought
Castile	watchful	poisoned
future	royal	against
half	focus	sole
Alfonso	ambitious	heir

ambitious: wanting to achieve the most or be successful *(adj.)*
poisoned: given a harmful substance that could be deadly *(v.)*
rewarded: given a prize for something well done *(v.)*
sole: only or single; one *(adj.)*
heir: someone who gets the property or title of a person who has died *(n.)*

Date: _____

2

cousin	nation	arranged
Ferdinand	marriage	heard
Aragón	territory	guards
vision	Portugal	servant
uniting	threatening	peril

royalty: kings, queens, and their families *(n.)*
territory: land *(n.)*
threatening: making statements that suggest harm *(v.)*
imprison: to put in a jail, prison, or dungeon *(v.)*
peril: danger *(n.)*

Date: _____

3

securing	supervised	assassin
armies	invasion	Granada
Moors	personally	Islam
although	specially	Jewish
pregnant	barely	convert

invade: to attack and enter a place with the plan to conquer it *(v.)*
assassin: murderer; someone who kills an important person *(n.)*
stronghold: fortress *(n.)*
convert: to change *(v.)*

Date: _____

4

Christopher	search	Americas
Columbus	India	provided
presented	finance	amount
lagged	voyage	resources
behind	genius	colonies

finance: to pay for *(v.)*
genius: incredibly smart *(adj.)*
resources: useful materials, such as gold or wood *(n.)*
colonies: groups of people that have moved to new lands and settled there, but are still considered a part of their home country; settlements *(n.)*

Date: _____

5

taught	clothes	proclaimed
palace	fanatical	natives
unified	millions	ignored
repaired	Inquisition	explorers
managing	dying	

unified: parts together as a whole; made into one *(adj.)*
repaired: fixed; made to work again *(v.)*
fanatical: overly excited about an idea; extreme *(adj.)*
proclaimed: announced or made known to the public *(v.)*
mistreated: acted badly toward, abused or harmed *(v.)*

Date: _____

Mark this Flight on your timeline:

| 1200 | 1300 | 1400 | 1450 | 1455 | 1460 | 1465 | 1470 | 1480 | 1490 | 1500 | 1510 | 1515 | 1520 |

Post-Flight Debriefing

Use your imagery to answer questions for the whole Flight:

A. What is the main idea for this Flight?

_____

_____

_____

B. Whom did Isabella choose to marry, and why?

    a) King Alfonso V of Portugal, because she was in love

    b) King Henry IV of Spain, to unite their countries

    c) Christopher Columbus, to support his voyage

    d) Prince Ferdinand of Aragón, to unite Spain

C. What impact did Isabella have during the Renaissance?

    a) She developed a unified code of laws.

    b) She financed Columbus' voyage to the New World.

    c) She started the Spanish Inquisition.

    d) all of the above

D. Why might Isabella have financed the voyage of an explorer like Columbus?

_____

_____

_____

Isabella waited nervously for Prince Ferdinand to arrive at her castle for their secret meeting. When she saw him...

_____

_____

_____

_____

_____

_____

_____

_____

_____

_____

_____

_____

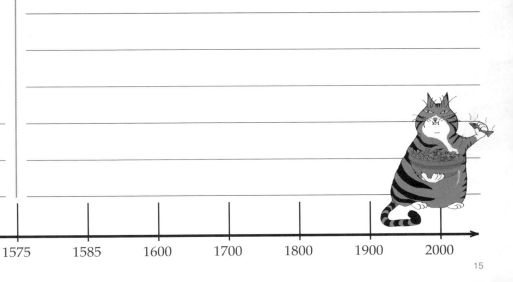

1530   1535   1540   1545   1550   1555   1565   1575   1585   1600   1700   1800   1900   2000

Flight 8

Pre-Flight for The Spanish Inquisition

Preread words for each paragraph:

Study and visualize the vocabulary:

1

Jews	practiced	pretended
unification	night	caught
Catholicism	bunkers	risk

Date: _____

punish: to harm or cause pain *(v.)*
unification: process of forming parts of something into one unit *(n.)*
practiced: acted out of habit or custom; followed *(v.)*
bunkers: protected rooms or sets of rooms built underground *(n.)*
homeland: the country where one was born or raised *(n.)*

2

advisors	crown	judges
true	highest	inquisitors
heretics	authority	systems
rules	permission	question
guessing	pious	

Date: _____

advisors: people who give advice to a leader *(n.)*
authority: a person or people in power *(n.)*
pope: the leader of the Catholic Church *(n.)*
pious: very religious *(adj.)*
inquisitors: people who investigate or question others *(n.)*

3

Torquemada	offenders	asked
raised	grace	differently
titles	period	including
humble	surrender	washed
organized	citizens	Saturdays

Date: _____

offenders: people who have committed a sin or crime *(n.)*
surrender: to give up; to turn yourself in to authorities *(v.)*
citizens: members of a state or nation *(n.)*
suspect: thought to be guilty *(adj.)*

4

cruel	presence	tortured
examined	frightened	horrible
heresy	confessed	executioners

Date: _____

confessed: admitted to a crime or sin *(v.)*
tortured: hurt someone to force them to do or say something *(v.)*
horrible: very bad; ugly; painful *(adj.)*
executioners: people who kill other people under order of a court or ruler *(n.)*

5

guilty	belongings	hunger
friends	outsiders	homelessness

Date: _____

guilty: judged to have committed a crime *(adj.)*
belongings: things that someone owns *(n.)*
branded: called, named, or labeled *(v.)*
outsiders: people who are not part of some group *(n.)*
homelessness: the state of having no place to live *(n.)*

Mark this Flight on your timeline:

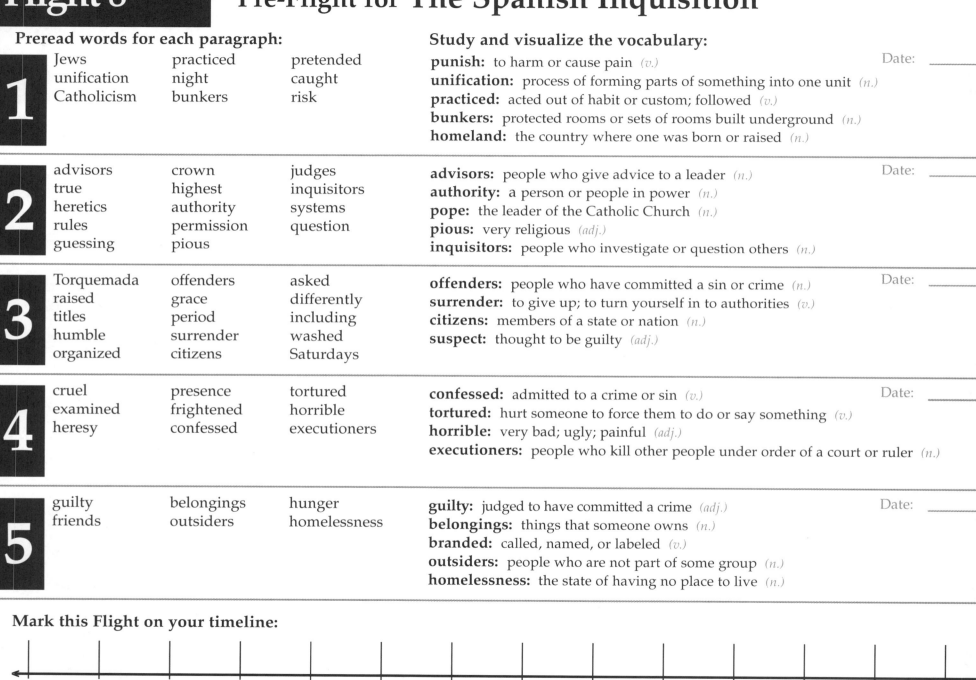

1200	1300	1400	1450	1455	1460	1465	1470	1480	1490	1500	1510	1515	1520

Post-Flight Debriefing

Date: _____

Use your imagery to answer questions for the whole Flight:

A. How would you summarize this Flight?

_____

_____

_____

B. The Spanish Inquisition persecuted all but which one of the following groups?

   a) Jews

   b) Catholics

   c) Non-Catholics

   d) Moors

C. Which of these is true about the Spanish Inquisition?

   a) Inquisitors were known to torture and punish suspected heretics.

   b) The Pope did not approve of the Inquisition.

   c) The Grand Inquisitor used his power to gain glory and riches.

   d) If a Muslim or Jew pretended to be Catholic, the Inquisition rewarded them.

D. Why do you think the Spanish Inquisition lasted for so long?

_____

_____

Write a Word Summary for the Spanish Inquisition.

_____

_____

_____

_____

_____

_____

_____

_____

_____

_____

_____

_____

_____

1530   1535   1540   1545   1550   1555   1565   1575   1585   1600   1700   1800   1900   2000

Flight 9

Pre-Flight for Columbus

Preread words for each paragraph:

Study and visualize the vocabulary:

Date: _____

1

wool	Atlantic	currents
join	ocean	supplies
Mediterranean	winds	

coast: seashore; land next to the sea *(n.)*
weaver: a person who makes fabrics from threads by crossing them over and under each other *(n.)*
currents: flows of water in certain directions *(n.)*
supplies: things needed, such as food and tools *(n.)*

Date: _____

2

eastern	actually	denied
veteran	quicker	request
round	certain	frustrated

veteran: a person who has had a lot of experience in a job *(n.)*
radical: extreme; unusual *(adj.)*
request: the act of asking for something *(n.)*
frustrated: kept from completing; made angry *(adj.)*

Date: _____

3

Perez	believing	crew
sheltered		

failed: did not succeed; was unable to complete or do *(adj.)*
bids: attempts or tries *(n.)*
sheltered: gave a place to live *(v.)*
plead: beg; to ask with a strong purpose *(v.)*
crew: sailors who work on a ship *(n.)*

Date: _____

4

August	months	accounting
Niña	sign	flying
Pinta	journals	island
Santa Maria	actual	calculations
enough	fictional	animals

journals: books with blank pages to write down notes; diaries *(n.)*
fictional: not real; made up *(adj.)*
lush: covered in growing plants *(adj.)*
calculations: results that have been gotten with careful planning and often math *(n.)*
holds: spaces in ships' bodies where cargo is held *(n.)*

Date: _____

5

San Salvador	cacao	correct
strangely	chocolate	otherwise
visitors	wheat	
language	prove	

sign language: a system of hand signals used to communicate *(n.)*
wheat: a grassy grain that is ground into flour and used to make bread *(n.)*
otherwise: differently; another way *(adv.)*

Mark this Flight on your timeline:

1200　1300　1400　1450　1455　1460　1465　1470　1480　1490　1500　1510　1515　1520

18

Post-Flight Debriefing

Use your imagery to answer questions for the whole Flight:

A. What is this Flight about?

_____

_____

_____

B. What was the error in Columbus' plan to sail to the East?

    a) He thought the East was actually in the South.
    b) He miscalculated the distance around the Earth.
    c) He underestimated the amount of food needed for the voyage.
    d) He thought that he could sail to the East in only a few days.

C. Who gave Columbus the money he needed for his voyage?

    a) King Alfonso V of Portugal
    b) Queen Elizabeth I of England
    c) Holy Roman Emperor Charles V
    d) Queen Isabella of Spain

D. Why do you think Columbus is famous even though he was wrong about his route to the Far East?

_____

_____

Columbus and his men pulled their small boats onto the white sand of the beach. They saw shadows moving in the jungle ahead and...

_____

_____

_____

_____

_____

_____

_____

_____

_____

_____

_____

_____

_____

| 1530 | 1535 | 1540 | 1545 | 1550 | 1555 | 1565 | 1575 | 1585 | 1600 | 1700 | 1800 | 1900 | 2000 |

Pre-Flight for Leonardo da Vinci

Preread words for each paragraph:

Study and visualize the vocabulary:

1

Leonardo	Verrocchio	antiques
da Vinci	architecture	beings
extra		

gifted: having skills or talents *(adj.)*
keen: sharp or strong *(adj.)*
architecture: the art of designing buildings *(n.)*
antiques: things that are very old and valuable *(n.)*

Date: _____

2

vegetarian	reptiles	quite
bought	dissected	chewed
caged	realistically	furniture
purpose	creatures	chaotic
wandered		

reptiles: cold-blooded animals with scales: snakes, lizards, etc. *(n.)*
dissected: cut apart in order to study *(v.)*
intent: focused on something *(adj.)*
creatures: different kinds of animals *(n.)*
chaotic: unorganized; very messy *(adj.)*

Date: _____

3

passionate	adopt	inspiration
enjoyed	orphaned	machines
patron	youth	

passionate: having strong feelings about something *(adj.)*
patron: someone who pays for the living expenses of an artist *(n.)*
adopt: to take care of as one's own, usually applied to children *(v.)*
orphaned: without parents *(adj.)*
inspiration: something that sparks an idea or action *(n.)*

Date: _____

4

monastery	recreate	viewed
Milan	arranging	stunned
sizing	disciples	applaud
looking	expressions	masterpiece
experiment		

monastery: a place where monks live *(n.)*
experiment: to test in order to learn something new *(v.)*
disciples: people who follow someone closely *(n.)*
expressions: the feelings shown on people's faces *(n.)*
masterpiece: the very best work of an artist; a work of the highest skill *(n.)*

Date: _____

5

touched	promised	rarely
blank	arrival	annoyed
Michelangelo	determination	aging
bare	succeed	

determination: a firm intent or sense of purpose *(n.)*
succeed: to finish something; to gain wealth or fame *(v.)*
rarely: not often *(adv.)*
aging: growing old *(adj.)*

Date: _____

Mark this Flight on your timeline:

| 1200 | 1300 | 1400 | 1450 | 1455 | 1460 | 1465 | 1470 | 1480 | 1490 | 1500 | 1510 | 1515 | 1520 |

Post-Flight Debriefing

Use your imagery to answer questions for the whole Flight:

A. What is the main idea for this Flight?

_____

_____

_____

B. Why did Leonardo da Vinci paint?

    a) for money

    b) because he loved it

    c) to free caged animals

    d) to prove he was better than Michelangelo

C. What did da Vinci do to learn how to sketch realistically?

    a) He followed people home and spied on them.

    b) He looked at and sketched all his relatives.

    c) He dissected dead animals.

    d) He studied medicine with famous doctors in Florence.

D. What things did Leonardo da Vinci do in his life that helped him become a great painter?

_____

_____

Based on your imagery, write a Picture Summary for this Flight.

_____

_____

_____

_____

_____

_____

_____

_____

_____

_____

_____

_____

_____

| 1530 | 1535 | 1540 | 1545 | 1550 | 1555 | 1565 | 1575 | 1585 | 1600 | 1700 | 1800 | 1900 | 2000 |

Pre-Flight for Leonardo the Inventor

Preread words for each paragraph:

Study and visualize the vocabulary:

1

inventor   capture   invention
uninterested

Date: _____

inventor: someone who creates something new *(n.)*
uninterested: paying no attention *(adj.)*
cameras: devices that take still pictures *(n.)*
capture: to catch and hold on to something *(v.)*

2

sketching   room   cloth
soar   pumped   helicopter

Date: _____

soar: fly high in the sky *(v.)*
cranks: handles on a machine that are turned to make the machine work *(n.)*
helicopter: a flying object that has no wings but uses rotating propellers to fly *(n.)*
blades: the flat and wide surfaces of an object *(n.)*
platform: a raised flat surface *(n.)*

3

cadavers   theorized   candlelight
exact   research   bodies
touching   model   x-rays
circulates

Date: _____

cadavers: dead bodies *(n.)*
internal: inside of something *(adj.)*
circulates: flows from place to place *(v.)*
theorized: came up with an idea based on observation *(v.)*
x-rays: pictures taken of the inside of a body without having to cut it open *(n.)*

4

engineer   developed   versions
Sforza   defense   tanks
weapons   value   advanced
advantage   weaponry

Date: _____

engineer: a person who plans and builds machines *(n.)*
advantage: a greater chance than someone else *(n.)*
weaponry: objects used in war to injure or kill *(n.)*
tanks: armored vehicles with guns that move along the ground on tracks *(n.)*
machine guns: guns that fire many bullets quickly when the trigger is pressed *(n.)*

5

weren't   backwards   clear
decades   mirror   wicked
massive   smear   observation

Date: _____

decades: time periods of ten years *(n.)*
massive: huge; a great amount *(adj.)*
wicked : mean or bad *(adj.)*
observation: power of seeing and noting things *(n.)*

Mark this Flight on your timeline:

1200   1300   1400   1450   1455   1460   1465   1470   1480   1490   1500   1510   1515   1520

Post-Flight Debriefing

Use your imagery to answer questions for the whole Flight:

A. What is the main idea for this Flight?

_____

_____

_____

B. What best describes Leonardo's interests?

    a) art, engineering, science, animals
    b) weapons, battle, engineering, fighting
    c) medicine, raising cows, architecture
    d) all of the above

C. Why did Leonardo want to learn and invent so much?

    a) He wanted to make his patron, the Duke of Milan, more powerful.
    b) He wanted to make money off of his inventions.
    c) He wanted to figure out a way to fly to the New World.
    d) He wanted to improve the world around him.

D. Why do you think Leonardo da Vinci is considered more than just a great painter?

_____

_____

_____

Tino was excited on his first day in Leonardo's workshop. He came through the door and was overwhelmed with the noise and smells. In the chaos, he suddenly...

_____

_____

_____

_____

_____

_____

_____

_____

_____

_____

_____

_____

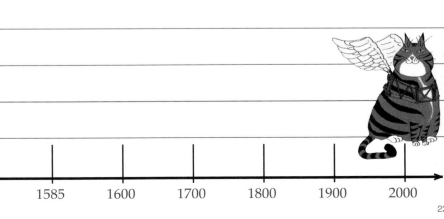

| 1530 | 1535 | 1540 | 1545 | 1550 | 1555 | 1565 | 1575 | 1585 | 1600 | 1700 | 1800 | 1900 | 2000 |

Flight 12

Pre-Flight for The Far East

Preread words for each paragraph:

Study and visualize the vocabulary:

1

spices	Genghis Khan	Ming Dynasty
existed	conquered	eventually
centuries	fierce	prosperity
brutal	warriors	porcelain
Mongols	overpowered	

Date: _____

conquered: took control by force; invaded *(v.)*
revolt: a fight against the leadership; a rebellion *(n.)*
prosperity: wealth in money and goods *(n.)*
silk: a fine, soft fabric made from the thread of silkworms *(n.)*
porcelain: a type of hard, white clay used as pottery *(n.)*

2

collection	Beijing	roofs
house	guests	fiery
emperor	outer	stood
capital		

Date: _____

emperor: the supreme ruler of a land or country *(n.)*
capital: the city where the head of government is *(n.)*
moat: a deep ditch filled with water around a fortress or castle *(n.)*
dragons: mythical monsters, like huge, fire-breathing lizards with wings *(n.)*
fiery: like fire; wild and hot *(adj.)*

3

export	strength	luxury
shiny	dishes	wealthiest
prized	vases	necessity
desirable	pottery	households
expensive		

Date: _____

export: something shipped or sold to another country *(n.)*
prized: wanted and valued highly *(adj.)*
desirable: extremely nice and worth having *(adj.)*
luxury: something that is costly but very nice to have *(n.)*
necessity: something that one cannot do without, like air or water *(n.)*

4

India	flavor	fragrant
local	peppercorns	oils
Mughal	ground	sandalwood
Arabian	cloves	applied
access	desserts	bathing

Date: _____

scattered: having parts in many different places; spread out *(adj.)*
peppercorns: the hard dry berries of the pepper plant *(n.)*
season: to add spices to make food more tasty *(v.)*
fragrant: having a nice smell *(adj.)*
oils: smooth, greasy liquids *(n.)*

5

Spice Islands	disliked	prices
arrogant	perfumes	source

Date: _____

minimal: a very small amount *(adj.)*
overland: on or across land *(adj.)*
arrogant: full of too much pride *(adj.)*
perfumes: liquids that smell very nice, worn on the body *(n.)*
bickering: arguing and fighting *(v.)*

Mark this Flight on your timeline:

```
◄———|——————|——————|——————|——————|——————|——————|——————|——————|——————|——————|——————|——————|——————
   1200   1300   1400   1450   1455   1460   1465   1470   1480   1490   1500   1510   1515   1520
```

24

Post-Flight Debriefing

Use your imagery to answer questions for the whole Flight:

A. What is the main concept for this Flight?

_____

_____

_____

B. What did the Ming Dynasty accomplish in China?

a) They developed trade along the Silk Road.
b) peace and prosperity
c) They built the Forbidden City.
d) all of the above

C. Which best describes trade items that people wanted from China?

a) animals, silk, and wood
b) spices, porcelain, and silk
c) furniture, spices, and perfume
d) oils, books, and spices

D. How do you think Europeans benefited from trade with the Far East?

_____

_____

_____

The weary traveler stepped from the ship onto the dock. He was in China for the first time. He needed to find food and a place to sleep, and then set up trade. He started...

_____

_____

_____

_____

_____

_____

_____

_____

_____

_____

_____

_____

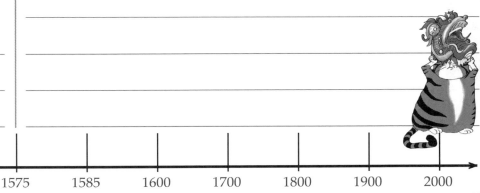

| 1530 | 1535 | 1540 | 1545 | 1550 | 1555 | 1565 | 1575 | 1585 | 1600 | 1700 | 1800 | 1900 | 2000 |

Flight 13

Pre-Flight for Vasco da Gama

Preread words for each paragraph:

Study and visualize the vocabulary:

Date: _____

1

flow	Vasco da Gama	raced
Portuguese	naval	toward
Manuel	officer	Africa
compete	attempt	

flow: a moving along from one place to another *(n.)*
naval: of a country's sailors and fighting ships *(adj.)*
officer: someone who is in command of others *(n.)*
Africa: the second largest continent, it is south of Europe *(n.)*

Date: _____

2

prepared	buy	further
vendors	fruit	guide
interested	vegetables	Calicut

prepared: made ready *(adj.)*
vendors: people who sell things *(n.)*
Calicut: a city on the coast of India which used to be a major center for trade and is known for its hand-woven cloth *(n.)*

Date: _____

3

expected	basins	emeralds
culture	honey	pearls
gifts	diamonds	insulted
custom	rubies	empty

custom: a practice or habit; an accepted way of doing things *(n.)*
basin: a bowl that holds liquids *(n.)*
honey: a thick and sweet liquid made by bees from the nectar of flowers *(n.)*
rubies: precious gems that are deep red in color *(n.)*
pearls: white, shiny, round gems made inside an oyster's shell *(n.)*

Date: _____

4

| scurvy | total | admiral |
| morale | success | |

scurvy: a disease caused by a lack of Vitamin C in the diet *(n.)*
morale: courage, confidence level *(n.)*
admiral: the leader of a navy *(n.)*

Date: _____

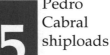

5

Pedro	agreements	sites
Cabral	forts	firmly
shiploads	key	established

fleet: a group of ships that sail together *(n.)*
key: important, having value *(adj.)*
sites: places *(n.)*
established: set up; founded; settled *(v.)*

Mark this Flight on your timeline:

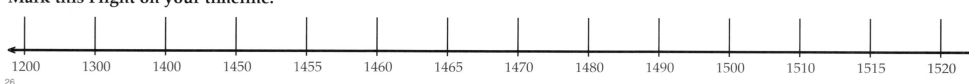

| 1200 | 1300 | 1400 | 1450 | 1455 | 1460 | 1465 | 1470 | 1480 | 1490 | 1500 | 1510 | 1515 | 1520 |

Post-Flight Debriefing

Use your imagery to answer questions for the whole Flight:

A. What was this Flight mainly about?

_____

_____

_____

B. Who controlled the flow of spices and goods from Asia in the 1400's?

a) Marco Polo
b) the Muslims
c) the Italians
d) all of the above

C. What did Vasco da Gama bring to trade with the natives of India?

a) emeralds, rubies, diamonds, and pearls
b) coffee beans, flour, and plums
c) hats, wash basins, beads, and honey
d) all of the above

D. Why do you think da Gama didn't succeed at setting up trade with India?

_____

_____

Vasco da Gama set his basket of beads down in front of the rich Indian ruler. The ruler looked at them and then...

_____

_____

_____

_____

_____

_____

_____

_____

_____

_____

_____

_____

| 1530 | 1535 | 1540 | 1545 | 1550 | 1555 | 1565 | 1575 | 1585 | 1600 | 1700 | 1800 | 1900 | 2000 |

Flight 14

Pre-Flight for The Explorers

Preread words for each paragraph:

Study and visualize the vocabulary:

1

Asia   launched   unsuccessful
forests   hopes

forests: lands covered with trees *(n.)*
stocked: loaded with or carrying *(adj.)*
launched: set off on a journey; set out to sea *(v.)*
unsuccessful: not able to do what was hoped for; failed *(adj.)*

Date: _____

2

Cabot   Canada   coastline
businessmen   mapped   announced
somewhere   rugged   headed

mapmaker: a person who makes accurate labeled drawings of places like oceans, lands, and coasts *(n.)*
rugged: rocky and uneven, often stormy *(adj.)*
coastline: the edge of the land, where it meets the sea *(n.)*

Date: _____

3

navigator   inspired   described
Amerigo   early   suggested
Vespucci

navigator: a person who plots the course or path of a ship *(n.)*
published: printed a large number of copies to be sold *(v.)*
suggested: told people about an idea *(v.)*

Date: _____

4

Juan   governor   source
Ponce de Leon   responsible   Florida
Hispaniola   rumored   brutalized
Puerto Rico   fountain   wounded

Puerto Rico: an island in the Caribbean Sea *(n.)*
governor: a person who rules a colony or province *(n.)*
eternal: without beginning or end; forever *(adj.)*
brutalized: treated with violence and cruelty; hurt *(v.)*
settlers: people who move to a new place and build the first houses, farms, or towns *(n.)*

Date: _____

5

Englishman   Carolinas   mutinied
north   tired   adrift
twice   starvation

Carolinas: rugged land on the eastern coast of North America *(n.)*
Hudson River: broad, beautiful river in present-day New York *(n.)*
bay: a wide area of the sea that is surrounded by land on three sides *(n.)*
mutinied: acted or fought against the captain's leadership *(v.)*
adrift: floating out of control *(adj.)*

Date: _____

Mark this Flight on your timeline:

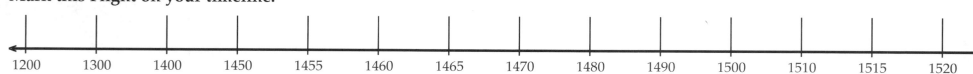

1200   1300   1400   1450   1455   1460   1465   1470   1480   1490   1500   1510   1515   1520

Post-Flight Debriefing

Use your imagery to answer questions for the whole Flight:

A. What is the main idea for this Flight?

_____

_____

_____

B. Who was placed in a boat and set adrift by his crew?

a) Vasco da Gama
b) John Cabot
c) Henry Hudson
d) Juan Ponce de Leon

C. Why did the New World come to be known as America?

a) It was named America by Christopher Columbus.
b) It was named America after Amerigo Vespucci.
c) It was named America after Henry Hudson.
d) It was named America by the American Indians.

D. Why might explorers have been so willing to risk their lives on dangerous voyages?

_____

_____

Cabot and his men peered at the newly discovered coastline ahead of them. They saw...

_____

_____

_____

_____

_____

_____

_____

_____

_____

_____

_____

_____

_____

1530 1535 1540 1545 1550 1555 1565 1575 1585 1600 1700 1800 1900 2000

Pre-Flight for Copernicus

Preread words for each paragraph:

Study and visualize the vocabulary:

1

Nikolaus	bright	Kraków
Copernicus	attended	decided
enrolled	university	income
shy		

Date: _____

middle-class: the level of people between the poor and the very wealthy, usually skilled workers or merchants *(adj.)*
enrolled: signed up, made a member *(v.)*
university: a college where people go to learn *(n.)*
Kraków: a city in Poland, a country that lies in the middle of Europe *(n.)*

2

professor	disapproved	earlier
avid	medicine	universe
astronomer	favorite	Ptolemy
observing	quiet	Aristotle
astronomy	studious	

Date: _____

professor: a high-ranking college teacher *(n.)*
avid: very eager or enthusiastic; devoted *(adj.)*
astronomer: a person who studies the sun, moon, and stars *(n.)*
medicine: the study of caring for and healing people who are sick *(n.)*
studious: fond of learning *(adj.)*

3

notebooks	addition	imprisoned
revolved	diocese	scholars
revolutionary	governed	

Date: _____

contradict: disagree with; oppose *(v.)*
revolutionary: something new and different that causes great change *(adj.)*
diocese: an area of land ruled by the Church and cared for by a bishop *(n.)*
bishop: a high Church leader in charge of a diocese *(n.)*
scholars: people who have studied and read a lot *(n.)*

4

rewriting	telescope	visual
theory	tool	mathematical
continually	rely	impossible
proof	naked	rumors

Date: _____

theory: an explanation for something based on facts and observation *(n.)*
orbits: the curved paths objects in space make around another object, such as planets around the sun *(n.)*
telescope: a device used to make far away objects seem closer and bigger *(n.)*

5

Rheticus	heliocentric	calm
convince	author	paralyzed
Revolutionibus	preface	meanwhile

Date: _____

heliocentric: with the sun as the center; the idea that the sun is at the center of the universe and the planets revolve around it *(adj.)*
preface: a written introduction or opening in a book *(n.)*
stroke: when a blood vessel breaks in the head and causes brain damage *(n.)*
paralyzed: unable to feel or move *(adj.)*

Mark this Flight on your timeline:

1200	1300	1400	1450	1455	1460	1465	1470	1480	1490	1500	1510	1515	1520

Post-Flight Debriefing

Use your imagery to answer questions for the whole Flight:

A. What is the main concept for this Flight?

_____

_____

_____

B. Who had a huge impact on Copernicus' future as an astronomer?

    a) his father
    b) a science teacher
    c) his uncle
    d) a math professor

C. Why didn't Copernicus publish his ideas until just before his death?

    a) He was unable to prove that his ideas were correct.
    b) He was ordered to keep silent by the King of Germany.
    c) He didn't want to share his ideas with everyone.
    d) He was completely opposed to being famous.

D. What was Copernicus' theory about the sun, Earth, and planets?

_____

_____

Write a Word Summary for this Flight.

_____

_____

_____

_____

_____

_____

_____

_____

_____

_____

_____

_____

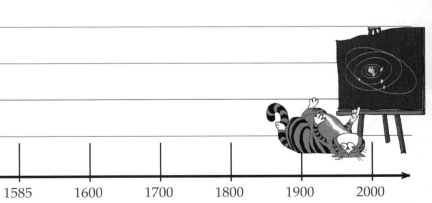

1530   1535   1540   1545   1550   1555   1565   1575   1585   1600   1700   1800   1900   2000

Pre-Flight for **Michelangelo**

Preread words for each paragraph:

Study and visualize the vocabulary:

1

Buonarroti | criticisms | direction
spoke | passionately | sculpting
shouts

dedicated: focused and committed to doing something *(adj.)*
criticisms: judgements or opinions about something *(n.)*
direction: instruction for doing something *(n.)*

Date: _____

2

village | pursue | stubbornness
stonecutters | uncertain | surprised
angry

stonecutters: people who cut blocks of stone out of the earth or carve stone for decoration *(n.)*
uncertain: not safe or dependable *(adj.)*
stubbornness: the state of being unwilling to change or stop *(n.)*
surprised: shocked and amazed *(v.)*

Date: _____

3

ego | embarrass | laughed
offended | asked | satisfied
distaste | quote | attitude
occasion | passage | Julius
bridge

ego: state of having too much pride and self-love *(n.)*
distaste: dislike or hatred *(n.)*
embarrass: to make someone feel stupid and shameful *(v.)*
quote: to repeat a passage or saying from memory *(v.)*
attitude: a way of treating other people and things; how a person expresses emotion *(n.)*

Date: _____

4

ceiling | entire | furious
newcomer | elated | backfired
jealous | hesitate | creating
special | Raphael
friendship

brash: rude and reckless in manners *(adj.)*
jealous: wanting what someone else has and disliking him/her for having it *(adj.)*
elated: very happy *(adj.)*
hesitate: to pause before acting, often due to fear or uncertainty *(v.)*
furious: very angry *(adj.)*

Date: _____

5

stood | apply | stretched
scaffold | section | figures
square | crouched | serious

scaffold: a platform on tall legs that stands high above the ground *(n.)*
square-yard: an area one yard (three feet) in length and one yard in width *(n.)*
plaster: a mixture put onto walls that is soft like paste when wet, but dries hard *(n.)*
watercolors: dry paints that are mixed with water for use in painting *(n.)*
serious: of great importance; painful and dangerous *(adj.)*

Date: _____

Mark this Flight on your timeline:

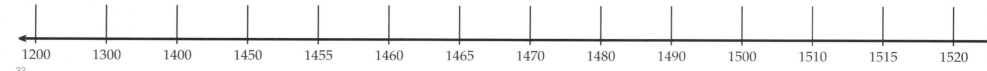

1200 1300 1400 1450 1455 1460 1465 1470 1480 1490 1500 1510 1515 1520

Post-Flight Debriefing

Use your imagery to answer questions for the whole Flight:

A. What is this Flight about?

_____

_____

_____

B. What famous painter did Michelangelo dislike?

a) Botticelli
b) Da Vinci
c) Verrocchio
d) Luigi

C. How did Michelangelo paint the ceiling of the Sistine Chapel?

a) by hanging from the ceiling from a rope and harness
b) by lying on his back on tall wooden scaffolds
c) by standing on a very tall ladder
d) by crouching on tall wooden scaffolds

D. Why do you think other painters of this time wanted Michelangelo to fail?

_____

_____

Michelangelo was painting. He crouched high on the scaffold, trying to see his paints and brushes by candlelight. Suddenly...

_____

_____

_____

_____

_____

_____

_____

_____

_____

_____

_____

_____

_____

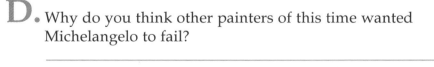

| 1530 | 1535 | 1540 | 1545 | 1550 | 1555 | 1565 | 1575 | 1585 | 1600 | 1700 | 1800 | 1900 | 2000 |

Preread words for each paragraph: **Study and visualize the vocabulary:**

1

Date: _____

marvel	decaying	remarkably
muscles	flesh	sculptures
corpses	caused	efforts
close		

marvel: something amazing *(n.)*
decaying: rotting *(adj.)*
flesh: the muscles and fat of a body that lie just under the skin *(n.)*
remarkably: worthy of notice; in an outstanding way *(adv.)*
sculptures: figures carved from materials such as clay, stone, or metal *(n.)*

2

Date: _____

La Pietà	smooth	chiseled
Jesus	St. Peter's	action
draped	piece	vowed
marble		

marble: hard rock that can be white or colored *(n.)*
St. Peter's Church: a large church in Rome, Italy *(n.)*
chiseled: cut or chipped away at wood or stone using a sharp pointed tool *(v.)*
rash: quick and without thought *(adj.)*
vowed: promised *(v.)*

3

Date: _____

David	accepted	shack
hero	imperfections	muscled

square: an open space at the center of a town or city where streets meet; plaza *(n.)*
task: a job or duty *(n.)*
imperfections: flaws or defects *(n.)*
muscled: very well built, as related to the body; strong *(adj.)*

4

Date: _____

chief	aching	hair
designer	frail	ruined
basilica	sparks	loneliness
ringing	precise	

designer: a person who plans and draws up ideas to be built *(n.)*
pained: caused hurt or suffering *(v.)*
aching: in constant pain *(adj.)*
frail: thin and weak *(adj.)*
precise: exact and accurate; perfect *(adj.)*

5

Date: _____

nephew	arrangements	respect
funeral	buried	traded

funeral: a ceremony held when a dead person is buried *(n.)*
arrangements: plans or preparations *(n.)*
thorny: difficult and annoying *(adj.)*
master: a leader; an expert *(n.)*

Mark this Flight on your timeline:

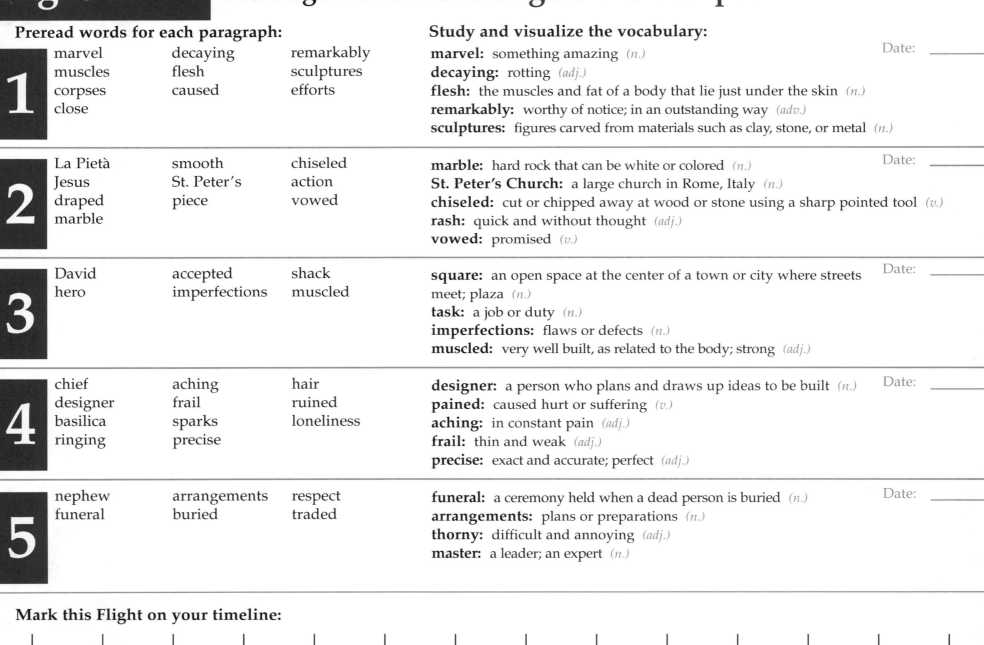

```
◄──┬────────┬────────┬────────┬────────┬────────┬────────┬────────┬────────┬────────┬────────┬────────┬────────┬────────┬──
  1200     1300     1400     1450     1455     1460     1465     1470     1480     1490     1500     1510     1515     1520
```

Post-Flight Debriefing

Use your imagery to answer questions for the whole Flight:

A. What is the main idea for this Flight?

_____

_____

_____

B. What hero from the Bible did Michelangelo sculpt a great statue of?

    a) Adam

    b) David

    c) Moses

    d) Solomon

C. What did Michelangelo study to learn how to sculpt the human body to look so real?

    a) anatomy books

    b) Leonardo da Vinci's sketchbooks

    c) corpses

    d) the poor

D. Why do you think Michelangelo felt so bad about chiseling his name on *La Pietà*?

_____

_____

Based on your imagery, write a Picture Summary for this Flight.

_____

_____

_____

_____

_____

_____

_____

_____

_____

_____

_____

_____

_____

_____

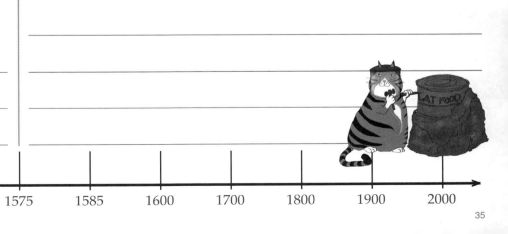

| 1530 | 1535 | 1540 | 1545 | 1550 | 1555 | 1565 | 1575 | 1585 | 1600 | 1700 | 1800 | 1900 | 2000 |

Pre-Flight for **Magellan**

Preread words for each paragraph:

Study and visualize the vocabulary:

1

Magellan	nautical	citizenship
parents	longed	

Date: _____

schooled: taught and trained *(v.)*
nautical: having to do with ships and sailors *(adj.)*
dishonored: shamed; made to lose honor or respect *(v.)*
citizenship: membership in a country that gives special status or privileges *(n.)*

2

Charles	hungry	captains
weather	mutiny	executed
scared	rebel	

Date: _____

passage: a way of going over or through something *(n.)*
bitter: harsh and unpleasant *(adj.)*
captains: the masters or leaders on ships *(n.)*
executed: killed for a purpose, usually legal *(v.)*

3

narrow	deserted	Pacifico
bottom	expedition	nothing
dangerous	November	nineteen
San Antonio	Mar	

Date: _____

deserted: left without warning or permission *(v.)*
expedition: a group on a journey or voyage *(n.)*
thrilled: excited and happy *(adj.)*
sawdust: fine particles of wood; the waste made when wood is sawed *(n.)*

4

kind	tribal	battle
Philippines	gratitude	arrow
Christianity	fight	

Date: _____

Philippines: a nation of many islands in the southwest Pacific *(n.)*
tribal: of or from a tribe *(adj.)*
gratitude: thankfulness *(n.)*
arrow: a wooden shaft with a sharp point, used as a weapon shot from a bow *(n.)*

5

sudden	del Cano	burned
command	April	September

Date: _____

loaded: filled with something *(v.)*
survived: remained alive afterward *(v.)*

Mark this Flight on your timeline:

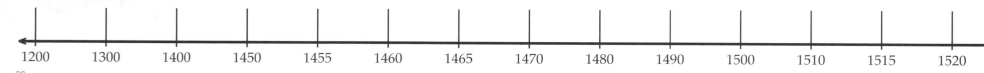

1200	1300	1400	1450	1455	1460	1465	1470	1480	1490	1500	1510	1515	1520

Post-Flight Debriefing

Date: _____

Use your imagery to answer questions for the whole Flight:

A. What is the main concept for this Flight?

_____

_____

_____

B. Where did Magellan arrive after sailing through the passage in South America?

   a) the Atlantic Ocean

   b) the Pacific Ocean

   c) the North Sea

   d) the Dead Sea

C. What did Magellan's men eat after they ran out of food?

   a) their shoes

   b) each other

   c) they didn't eat anything

   d) rats and sawdust

D. Why do you think Magellan is still considered the first man to sail around the world, even though he died on his great voyage?

_____

_____

The ship floated still in the water. They had been at sea for days with no sign of land. Suddenly they saw...

_____

_____

_____

_____

_____

_____

_____

_____

_____

_____

_____

_____

1530	1535	1540	1545	1550	1555	1565	1575	1585	1600	1700	1800	1900	2000

Flight 19

Pre-Flight for Raphael

Preread words for each paragraph:

Study and visualize the vocabulary:

1

Santi   intellectuals   central
Urbino   teenager   errands
collector   Perugino

Urbino: a town in central Italy *(n.)*
collector: a person who gathers something *(n.)*
intellectuals: great thinkers *(n.)*
errands: simple everyday jobs or tasks *(n.)*

Date: _____

2

imitated   rivals   Madonnas
surpassed   delicacy   perfection
idolized   especially   uniquely

imitated: copied, followed the example of *(v.)*
surpassed: became better than; went beyond *(v.)*
idolized: looked up to, admired, adored *(v.)*
rivals: people who want to be better than each other at some task *(n.)*
delicacy: fineness; precision and care *(n.)*

Date: _____

3

modest   Plato   hugely
financial   forum   Bolsena
Athens   Greece

modest: not full of pride; not thinking highly of one's self *(adj.)*
financial: of or about money *(adj.)*
blossomed: developed into; grew *(v.)*
forum: an area in an ancient Roman city where people would gather to shop, do business, and have meetings *(n.)*

Date: _____

4

height   attain   assistants
unveiled   tapestries   incredibly
shattered   Leo   polite
possesses   despite   exhaustion
endeavor   rely

unveiled: uncovered, revealed, or made known *(v.)*
self-confidence: belief in one's own abilities *(n.)*
endeavor: try hard; make an effort *(v.)*
attain: reach or get *(v.)*
exhaustion: the state of being very tired and worn out *(n.)*

Date: _____

5

engaged   straight   transfiguration
daughter   fever   pupil
none   birthday   wept

engaged: promised to be married *(adj.)*
fever: when the body's temperature is too high, usually as a result of sickness *(n.)*
pupil: a student; someone who is learning *(n.)*
wept: cried or shed tears *(v.)*

Date: _____

Mark this Flight on your timeline:

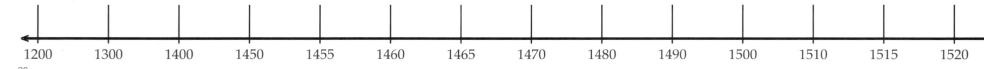

1200   1300   1400   1450   1455   1460   1465   1470   1480   1490   1500   1510   1515   1520

Post-Flight Debriefing

Use your imagery to answer questions for the whole Flight:

A. How would you summarize this Flight?

_____

_____

_____

B. Why was Raphael sent to live with Perugino?

a) Perugino was his uncle and Raphael was an orphan.
b) to learn how to build churches
c) because Michelangelo refused to take Raphael in
d) to develop his amazing talent as a painter

C. Who influenced young Raphael's painting?

a) Michelangelo and Leonardo da Vinci
b) Leonardo da Vinci and Botticelli
c) no one
d) Botticelli and Michelangelo

D. Why might it be considered tragic that Raphael died so young?

_____

_____

Write a Word Summary for what you know about Raphael.

_____

_____

_____

_____

_____

_____

_____

_____

_____

_____

_____

_____

_____

| 1530 | 1535 | 1540 | 1545 | 1550 | 1555 | 1565 | 1575 | 1585 | 1600 | 1700 | 1800 | 1900 | 2000 |

Pre-Flight for Martin Luther

Preread words for each paragraph:

Study and visualize the vocabulary:

Date: _____

1

Martin	quit	terror
Luther	event	stricken
Germany	severe	overwhelmed
college	lightning	involuntary
lawyer	companion	

severe: intense; very bad *(adj.)*
companion: a friend; a person who travels with another *(n.)*
overwhelmed: crushed and conquered *(v.)*
impending: about to happen *(adj.)*
involuntary: not done by choice *(adj.)*

Date: _____

2

fulfilled	insomnia	indulgences
monastery	appalled	purchaser
expert	superiors	forgiven
firsthand		

fulfilled: happy; at ease; having no cares *(adj.)*
insomnia: a state of not being able to fall asleep *(n.)*
appalled: shocked and disgusted *(adj.)*
superiors: people of higher rank *(n.)*

Date: _____

3

salvation	objections	excitement
concerned	debate	anger
officials	folk	mobbed
ninety-five	generating	bonfire
theses		

salvation: the Christian idea of saving the soul from sin; rescue *(n.)*
lavish: rich and wasteful *(adj.)*
officials: people who hold positions of power in a group *(n.)*
objections: disagreements or complaints *(n.)*
debate: discussion or argument about something *(v.)*

Date: _____

4

riots	divide	absent
kicked	fugitive	iniquity
practices		

shopkeepers: merchants who sell goods in a shop *(n.)*
riots: large angry groups of people that become violent *(n.)*
fugitive: a person running from danger or the law *(n.)*
absent: not there; not present *(adj.)*
iniquity: wickedness; evil; sin *(n.)*

Date: _____

5

excommunicated	common	intention
exiled	corrupt	basis
dreary	anniversary	Protestant
miserable	truce	

exiled: forced to leave a group or place *(v.)*
dreary: damp, windy, and cold; dark and unpleasant *(adj.)*
corrupt: gaining benefits from giving unearned favors or votes *(adj.)*
anniversary: the date of some event which happens once per year *(n.)*
truce: an agreement to stop fighting *(n.)*

Mark this Flight on your timeline:

1200	1300	1400	1450	1455	1460	1465	1470	1480	1490	1500	1510	1515	1520

Post-Flight Debriefing

Use your imagery to answer questions for the whole Flight:

A. What is the main idea for this Flight?

_____

_____

_____

B. What event led Luther to become a priest?

    a) getting kicked out of law school
    b) meeting and marrying a beautiful woman
    c) getting caught in a fierce lightning storm that killed his friend
    d) visiting the corrupt Church leaders in Rome

C. Why did Luther nail his paper to the church door?

    a) to make sure that the local priests saw it
    b) it was where public notices were posted
    c) He couldn't get it to the newspaper office in time.
    d) He wanted to make sure no one saw it.

D. Why do you think Martin Luther's ideas generated so much excitement and anger?

_____

_____

Luther finished hanging his paper on the church door. People crowded around to read it. Then they began to talk about Luther's paper. They said…

_____

_____

_____

_____

_____

_____

_____

_____

_____

_____

_____

_____

_____

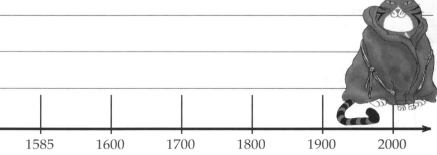

1530	1535	1540	1545	1550	1555	1565	1575	1585	1600	1700	1800	1900	2000

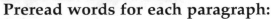

Flight 21

Pre-Flight for Henry VIII

Preread words for each paragraph:

Study and visualize the vocabulary:

1

Arthur	playing	stable
outdoors	singer	treasury

Date: _____

hunting: catching and killing animals for sport or to eat as food *(v.)*
stable: steady; secure *(adj.)*
treasury: a place where money is kept *(n.)*

2

government	Wolsey	France
duties	advice	navy
cardinal		

Date: _____

government: the system for making the laws for a country *(n.)*
duties: jobs; tasks *(n.)*
cardinal: a person with high rank in the Church *(n.)*
advice: encouragement or helpful ideas for how one should act *(n.)*
navy: a country's fighting ships and sailors *(n.)*

3

tearing	strengthen	Boleyn
Catherine	alliance	divorce
Aragón	Anne	

Date: _____

strengthen: to make more powerful; to make stronger *(v.)*
alliance: the joining of nations for a common goal *(n.)*
divorce: the ending of a marriage by law *(n.)*

4

questioning	headstrong	beheaded
prone	Elizabeth	eleven
rage	adultery	Seymour
scandal		

Date: _____

attacking: fighting or arguing against; fighting using force *(v.)*
prone: likely to say or do something *(adj.)*
treason: turning against a country or leader; to help an enemy instead of an ally *(n.)*
scandal: something that brings disgrace or dishonor *(n.)*
beheaded: killed by cutting the head off *(v.)*

5

devastated	ugly	Edward
perhaps	Howard	replacement
truly	marrying	inherited
Cleves		

Date: _____

devastated: destroyed; filled with grief *(v.)*
deemed: believed; thought; passed judgement on *(v.)*
replacement: a person who fills or takes the place of another; a substitute *(n.)*
crowned: given the throne; made a king or queen *(v.)*
inherited: got something after the owner died; was left with *(v.)*

Mark this Flight on your timeline:

| 1200 | 1300 | 1400 | 1450 | 1455 | 1460 | 1465 | 1470 | 1480 | 1490 | 1500 | 1510 | 1515 | 1520 |

Post-Flight Debriefing

Use your imagery to answer questions for the whole Flight:

A. What is the main concept for this Flight?

_____

_____

_____

B. Which of these best describes the life of Henry VIII?

　　a) He was an intelligent king, famous for his love of music and hunting.
　　b) He became the king of Egypt when he was a young man.
　　c) He was a brave king, known for conquering France and Germany.
　　d) He was known for having eight wives.

C. Why did Henry create a church to replace the Roman Catholic Church?
　　a) He wanted a church that would not allow divorce.
　　b) He wanted the Catholic Church's land and money.
　　c) He was angry when the Catholic Church opposed his divorce.
　　d) Henry didn't replace the Catholic Church.

D. Why do you think that Henry married so many times? Explain.

_____

_____

Ned was excited to be serving dinner in King Henry's main dining room. He carried a steaming platter as he entered, trying to see everything at once. Suddenly, he...

_____

_____

_____

_____

_____

_____

_____

_____

_____

_____

_____

_____

1530　1535　1540　1545　1550　1555　1565　1575　1585　1600　1700　1800　1900　2000

Flight 22

Pre-Flight for Nostradamus

Preread words for each paragraph:

Study and visualize the vocabulary:

1

Nostradamus	predict	patients
physician	cure	suggest
astrologer	seriously	grief

Date: _____

physician: a doctor of medicine *(n.)*
predict: to say what will happen before it happens *(v.)*
patients: the sick or hurt people that a doctor helps *(n.)*
unable: not skilled enough *(adj.)*
grief: a great feeling of sadness and pain, caused by loss *(n.)*

2

| beard | visions | predictions |
| miracles | trance | |

Date: _____

balding: losing the hair on the head *(adj.)*
miracles: fantastic acts or healing that cannot be explained *(n.)*
visions: pictures or images *(n.)*
trance: a dreamy daze *(n.)*

3

popularity	quatrains	sure
rhyming	confuse	exactly
verse		

Date: _____

rhyming: repeating the same sounds in different words, usually at the ends of lines in poems *(adj.)*
verse: a section of poetry *(n.)*
quatrains: lines of a poem that are put together in groups of four *(n.)*
confuse: to make unclear; to mix up or keep someone from understanding *(v.)*

4

| forebodings | introduced | decision |
| parties | | |

Date: _____

forebodings: predictions; things that are known about and spoken of before they actually happen *(n.)*
introduced: presented to another for the first time *(v.)*
witch: a person thought to have wicked magical powers; a servant of Satan *(n.)*

5

| crippling | horoscopes | Kennedy |
| arthritis | clients | |

Date: _____

arthritis: a disease that causes pain in the joints of the body *(n.)*
bedridden: not able to get out of bed *(adj.)*
claim: to state with force; to believe *(v.)*
World War II: a war that lasted from 1939 to 1945 involving America & Europe *(n.)*
John F. Kennedy: the 35th American president, assassinated in 1963 *(n.)*

Mark this Flight on your timeline:

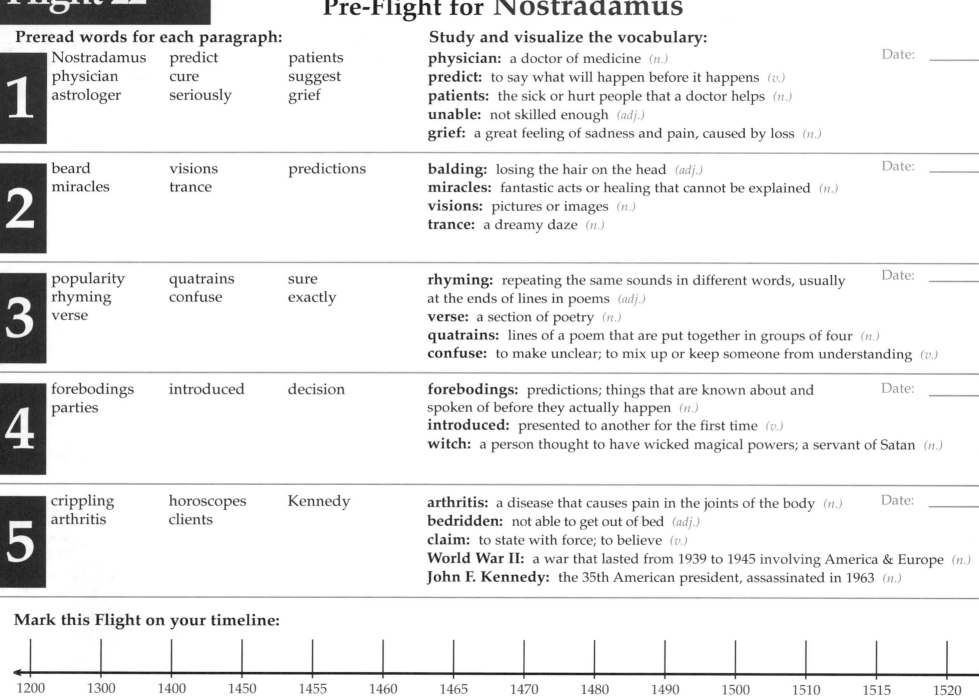

1200   1300   1400   1450   1455   1460   1465   1470   1480   1490   1500   1510   1515   1520

Post-Flight Debriefing

Use your imagery to answer questions for the whole Flight:

A. What is this Flight about?

_____

_____

_____

B. What did Nostradamus do for a living?

    a) He was an advisor to the King of France.

    b) He was a dentist.

    c) He was a lawyer.

    d) He was a physician.

C. Which of these describes Nostradamus' book *Centuries*?

    a) It is very difficult to read and understand.

    b) It consists of Nostradamus' predictions and visions of the future.

    c) Nostradamus wrote it in rhyming verse in four languages.

    d) all of the above

D. Why do you think Nostradamus' book *Centuries* became so popular?

_____

_____

Nostradamus was helping the sick man drink his medicine when someone pounded at the door. Scared that the Inquisition had found him, he...

_____

_____

_____

_____

_____

_____

_____

_____

_____

_____

_____

_____

_____

_____

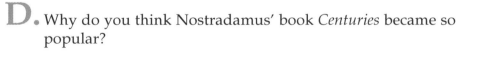

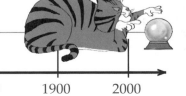

1530   1535   1540   1545   1550   1555   1565   1575   1585   1600   1700   1800   1900   2000

Pre-Flight for Bloody Mary

Preread words for each paragraph: **Study and visualize the vocabulary:**

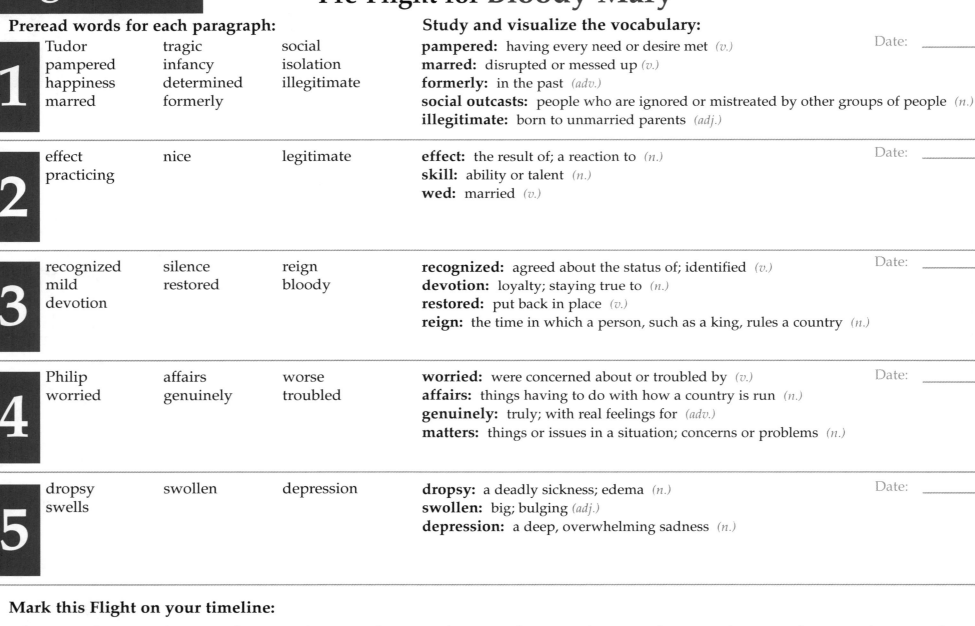

1

Tudor	tragic	social
pampered	infancy	isolation
happiness	determined	illegitimate
marred	formerly	

Date: _____

pampered: having every need or desire met *(v.)*
marred: disrupted or messed up *(v.)*
formerly: in the past *(adv.)*
social outcasts: people who are ignored or mistreated by other groups of people *(n.)*
illegitimate: born to unmarried parents *(adj.)*

2

effect	nice	legitimate
practicing		

Date: _____

effect: the result of; a reaction to *(n.)*
skill: ability or talent *(n.)*
wed: married *(v.)*

3

recognized	silence	reign
mild	restored	bloody
devotion		

Date: _____

recognized: agreed about the status of; identified *(v.)*
devotion: loyalty; staying true to *(n.)*
restored: put back in place *(v.)*
reign: the time in which a person, such as a king, rules a country *(n.)*

4

Philip	affairs	worse
worried	genuinely	troubled

Date: _____

worried: were concerned about or troubled by *(v.)*
affairs: things having to do with how a country is run *(n.)*
genuinely: truly; with real feelings for *(adv.)*
matters: things or issues in a situation; concerns or problems *(n.)*

5

dropsy	swollen	depression
swells		

Date: _____

dropsy: a deadly sickness; edema *(n.)*
swollen: big; bulging *(adj.)*
depression: a deep, overwhelming sadness *(n.)*

Mark this Flight on your timeline:

| 1200 | 1300 | 1400 | 1450 | 1455 | 1460 | 1465 | 1470 | 1480 | 1490 | 1500 | 1510 | 1515 | 1520 |

Post-Flight Debriefing

Use your imagery to answer questions for the whole Flight:

A. What is the main idea for this Flight?

_____

_____

_____

B. What did Mary accomplish during her rule of England?

a) She had a son that took the English throne after her death.
b) She restored the Catholic Church in England and charged Protestants with heresy.
c) She asked her beloved sister Elizabeth to rule by her side.
d) She lived a long and healthy life.

C. Why did Mary wed Prince Philip II of Spain?

a) He promised to give her the Spanish lands in the New World.
b) He was Catholic, and she wanted to have a child with him.
c) Her sister Elizabeth loved him, and Mary wanted to make her jealous.
d) all of the above

D. Why do you think Mary was not popular with her people?

_____

_____

Write a Word Summary for this Flight.

_____

_____

_____

_____

_____

_____

_____

_____

_____

_____

_____

_____

_____

1530 1535 1540 1545 1550 1555 1565 1575 1585 1600 1700 1800 1900 2000

Flight 24

Pre-Flight for Conquest of Mesoamerica

Preread words for each paragraph: **Study and visualize the vocabulary:**

1

civilizations	Mesoamerican	wiped
advances	Aztecs	victims
engineering	Incas	

well-developed: complex *(adj.)*
civilizations: cultures that typically have law, government, written language, art, and music *(n.)*
rivaled: competed with; compared to *(v.)*
superior: better; more powerful *(adj.)*

Date: _____

2

Mexico	enormous	captives
swampland	temples	sacrificed
swamps	restricted	crops
canals	elite	slaves
pyramids		

gleaming: bright and shining *(adj.)*
canals: man-made waterways *(n.)*
elite: a top and select group; the very best *(adj.)*
captives: people seized in war; prisoners *(n.)*
sacrifices: offerings to the gods *(n.)*

Date: _____

3

conquistador	unsatisfied	destroyed
Cortés	confusion	germs
Montezuma	jewels	

conquistador: a Spanish soldier who was also an explorer *(n.)*
kidnapped: stole; carried off, or abducted by force *(v.)*
jewels: gems and stones of great value *(n.)*
germs: tiny living things that get in the human body and make people sick *(n.)*

Date: _____

4

mountains	slide	snaked
Peru	fixed	terraces
fortresses	cobblestone	irrigation

slide: to move downward; to move smoothly *(v.)*
cobblestone: naturally rounded stones, used in paving roads *(n.)*
snaked: turned back and forth in a curvy, winding path *(v.)*
terraces: strips of flat land cut out of a slope that resemble stairs *(n.)*
irrigation: a system used to supply water to dry land *(n.)*

Date: _____

5

population	Pizarro	knives
Spaniard	Atahuallpa	swords
Francisco	ransom	

ransom: the amount paid to free a prisoner *(n.)*
clubs: short thick pieces of wood used to hit or beat *(n.)*
swords: metal weapons, usually flat and straight with sharp edges *(n.)*

Date: _____

Mark this Flight on your timeline:

1200   1300   1400   1450   1455   1460   1465   1470   1480   1490   1500   1510   1515   1520

48

Post-Flight Debriefing

Date: _____

Use your imagery to answer questions for the whole Flight:

A. How would you summarize this Flight?

_____

_____

_____

B. What were the two most advanced civilizations the Spanish found in the New World?

   a) the Indians and the Aztecs

   b) the Aztecs and the Incas

   c) the Incas and the Indians

   d) the Incas and the Perus

C. What was responsible for wiping out the natives?

   a) guns

   b) disease

   c) conquistadors

   d) all of the above

D. Why do you think the Aztec and Incan civilizations were considered to be advanced?

_____

_____

_____

Tico rode his horse at the front of the conquistador army. As he entered the Aztec city, he was amazed by...

_____

_____

_____

_____

_____

_____

_____

_____

_____

_____

_____

_____

_____

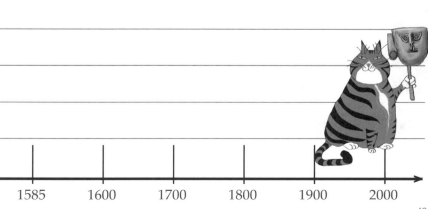

1530	1535	1540	1545	1550	1555	1565	1575	1585	1600	1700	1800	1900	2000

Flight 25

Pre-Flight for Ivan the Terrible

Preread words for each paragraph:

Study and visualize the vocabulary:

1

Vasilyevich	Julius	boyars
czar	Caesar	eight
Russia		

Date: _____

czar: the emperor of Russia *(n.)*
Russia: also called the Russian Empire, an empire that lasted until 1917 *(n.)*
Julius Caesar: a Roman general (c. 100-44 B.C.) who rose in power to become one of the greatest leaders of Rome *(n.)*
boyars: Russian nobles or lords *(n.)*

2

abused	kitchen	glamour
neglected	amidst	grozny

Date: _____

neglected: ignored; gave no care to *(v.)*
glamour: beauty and excitement *(n.)*
harsh: severe; causing pain or irritation *(adj.)*
grozny: Russian word that means awesome or terrible *(adj.)*

3

actively	collapse	oprichniki
Anastasia	paranoid	innocent
Romanov	extreme	drowned
relatively	suspicious	hanged
corruption	soldiers	

Date: _____

corruption: misusing a job or trust for personal gain; dishonesty *(n.)*
paranoid: being overly mistrusting; suspecting others without reason *(adj.)*
suspicious: distrustful; wary; having doubt *(adj.)*
plotters: people planning together in secret *(n.)*
lashing: physically or verbally attacking *(v.)*

4

failure	argument	heavy
terrified	angrily	coma

Date: _____

terrified: very scared; filled with great fear or horror *(v.)*
argument: disagreement or verbal fight *(n.)*
staff: a walking stick or cane *(n.)*
coma: a medical condition like a long deep sleep *(n.)*
sanity: mental health; well being of the mind *(n.)*

5

seesawing	moody	handicapped
regret	shoulder	remove

Date: _____

seesawing: going back and forth; changing one's mind a lot *(v.)*
gain: to get or earn *(v.)*
mentally-handicapped: disabled in the mind *(adj.)*
crumble: fall apart; break into pieces *(v.)*

Mark this Flight on your timeline:

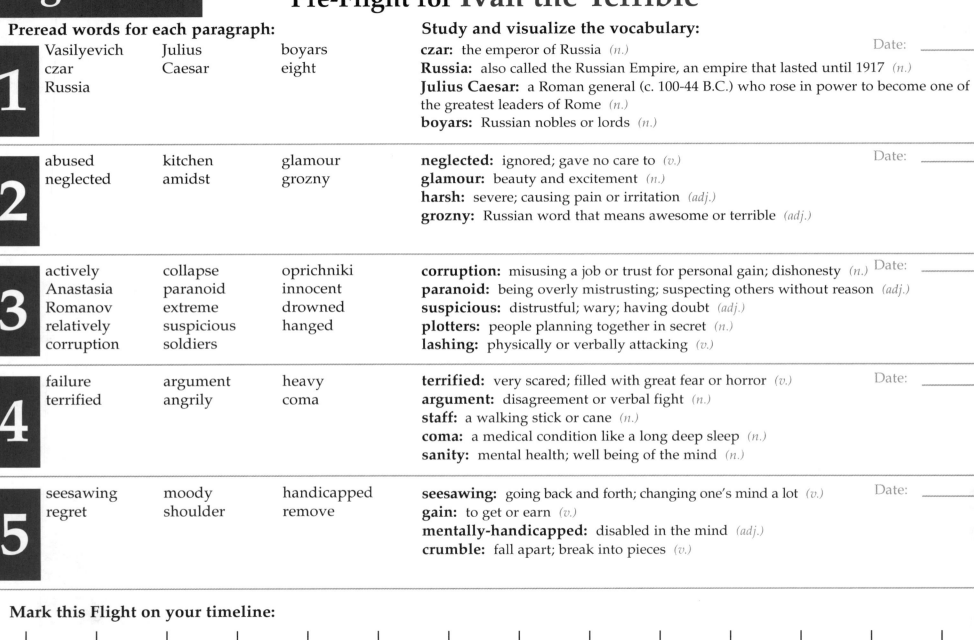

1200   1300   1400   1450   1455   1460   1465   1470   1480   1490   1500   1510   1515   1520

Post-Flight Debriefing

Use your imagery to answer questions for the whole Flight:

A. What is this Flight about?

_____

_____

_____

B. What did Ivan do when he felt regret over his harsh actions?

a) He formed a secret elite force.
b) He had himself arrested, tried, and convicted for his crimes.
c) He spent hours praying for forgiveness.
d) He apologized to everyone involved.

C. What was the name of the elite force Ivan created?

a) Persnicketys
b) Russian Army
c) Oprichniki
d) none of the above

D. Why was Ivan known as "Ivan the Terrible?"

_____

_____

Young Ivan held his little brother's hand as they snuck down the dark palace hall together. They had just crept into the empty kitchen when...

_____

_____

_____

_____

_____

_____

_____

_____

_____

_____

_____

_____

_____

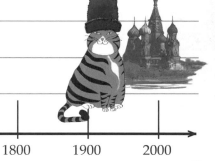

| 530 | 1535 | 1540 | 1545 | 1550 | 1555 | 1565 | 1575 | 1585 | 1600 | 1700 | 1800 | 1900 | 2000 |

Flight 26

Pre-Flight for Elizabeth I

Preread words for each paragraph:

Study and visualize the vocabulary:

1

red-haired   largely   empty

care: attention and help *(n.)*

Date: _____

2

thirteen   London   relations
tower   diplomacy   ascended

Tower of London: a historic fortress used as a prison *(n.)*
diplomacy: skill in handling relationships between countries or nations *(n.)*
petty: unimportant; trivial *(adj.)*
ascended: rose; went up *(v.)*

Date: _____

3

immediately   pushed   ceremony
shutting   teased   inspiring
replacing   certain   spectacle

finest: best; most luxurious *(adj.)*
teased: pulled and puffed hair with a comb *(v.)*
painted: put a lot of makeup on *(v.)*
ceremony: a formal or special event *(n.)*
spectacle: an unusual or uncommon sight *(n.)*

Date: _____

4

Protestantism   galleons   attempted
expansion   pirates   knock
mighty   harassed   network

exploration: a journey of discovery; a search *(n.)*
expansion: an increase or enlargement *(n.)*
galleons: large sailing ships of the 15th to 17th centuries, usually used for fighting *(n*
harassed: criticized, bothered, or attacked again and again *(v.)*
network: an organized group; a web or system of people *(n.)*

Date: _____

5

economic   historian   sighing
flourishing   Stow   hath
theater   general

flourishing: growing rich or strong *(v.)*
theater: a building used for shows or plays, with seats and a stage *(n.)*
historian: a person who studies, teaches, or writes about history *(n.)*
groaning: making a deep sound to show pain or sadness *(v.)*
hath: a form of the modern word 'has' *(v.)*

Date: _____

Mark this Flight on your timeline:

| 1200 | 1300 | 1400 | 1450 | 1455 | 1460 | 1465 | 1470 | 1480 | 1490 | 1500 | 1510 | 1515 | 1520 |

Post-Flight Debriefing

Use your imagery to answer questions for the whole Flight:

A. What is the main idea for this Flight?

_____

_____

_____

B. Which of these was NOT a reason why Elizabeth's rule was unique?

   a) She was a woman.

   b) She was born in France.

   c) She never married.

   d) She was once considered illegitimate.

C. Which of these best describes Elizabeth I?

   a) She loved the arts and encouraged exploration and expansion.

   b) She was a devout Catholic.

   c) She made sure the spies of her spy network were paid well.

   d) She married young and had a son.

D. How might Elizabeth's love of arts and education have changed people's lives?

_____

_____

The young actor was thrilled about his chance to act in a play for Good Queen Bess. As he walked onto the stage and stood before her, there was a sudden...

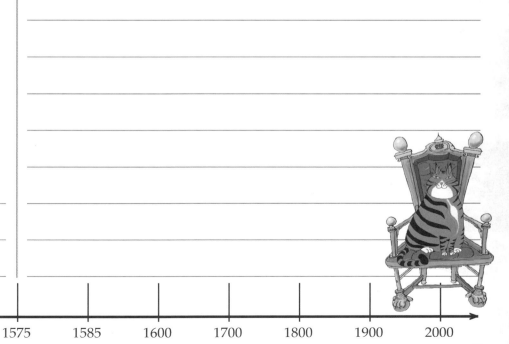

530	1535	1540	1545	1550	1555	1565	1575	1585	1600	1700	1800	1900	2000

Flight 27

Pre-Flight for Sir Francis Drake

Preread words for each paragraph:

Study and visualize the vocabulary:

1

Francis	daring	revenge
Hawkins	West Indies	

daring: brave; risky *(adj.)*
slave-trading: in the business of catching and shipping people to be sold as slaves *(adj*
West Indies: a group of islands in the Caribbean Sea known for their spices *(n.)*
revenge: a plan to hurt someone in repayment for a wrong *(n.)*

2

privateer	treasure	unguarded
settlements	llamas	jungle
mine	camel	

privateer: a privately-owned ship, hired by a country to fight *(n.)*
settlements: small new towns where people have decided to live *(n.)*
mine: a hole made in the ground to dig up minerals *(n.)*
unguarded: without any protection *(adj.)*
llamas: South American animals that look like shaggy camels without humps *(n.)*

3

approved	blown	lead
tense	course	Golden Hind

approved: okayed; consented to *(v.)*
relations: friendships or conditions between *(n.)*
tense: nervous; jumpy; strained *(adj.)*
course: a planned route *(n.)*
lead: the one in front; main or most important *(adj.)*

4

stole	newly	adventure
docked		

raided: attacked without warning *(v.)*
stole: took without permission *(v.)*
docked: approached and then tied a ship up to a dock *(v.)*
newly-claimed: just now taken possession of *(adj.)*

5

sir	harbor	mourned
Armada	victor	dear
readying	harassing	

demanded: commanded; asked for very strongly *(v.)*
readying: preparing *(v.)*
harbor: a port; a place where ships gather *(n.)*
victor: the winner *(n.)*
mourned: grieved; felt sad for *(v.)*

Mark this Flight on your timeline:

1200	1300	1400	1450	1455	1460	1465	1470	1480	1490	1500	1510	1515	1520

Post-Flight Debriefing

Use your imagery to answer questions for the whole Flight:

Write a Word Summary for Sir Francis Drake.

A. What is the main concept for this Flight?

_____

_____

_____

B. Why did the Spanish hate Francis Drake?

  a) He had taken their land in the New World away.
  b) He had raced their ships to the New World and won.
  c) He had advised Elizabeth not to marry the King of Spain.
  d) He had stolen from their ships.

C. What was the name of Drake's lead ship?

  a) *Privateer*
  b) *Golden Hind*
  c) *Constitution*
  d) *Santa Maria*

D. Why do you think Queen Elizabeth liked Drake so much?

_____

_____

_____

| 1530 | 1535 | 1540 | 1545 | 1550 | 1555 | 1565 | 1575 | 1585 | 1600 | 1700 | 1800 | 1900 | 2000 |

Pre-Flight for Spanish Armada

Preread words for each paragraph: **Study and visualize the vocabulary:**

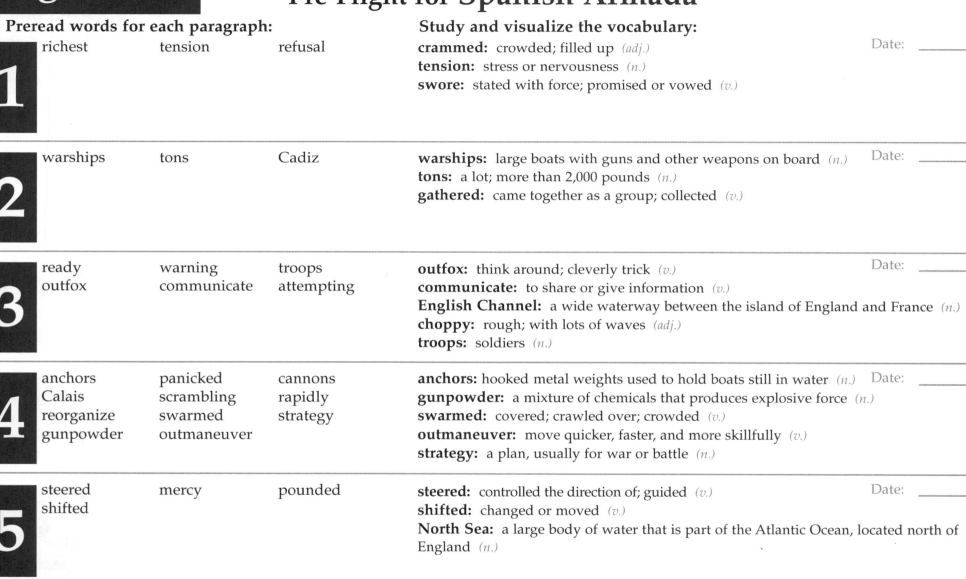

1

| richest | tension | refusal |

Date: _____

crammed: crowded; filled up *(adj.)*
tension: stress or nervousness *(n.)*
swore: stated with force; promised or vowed *(v.)*

2

| warships | tons | Cadiz |

Date: _____

warships: large boats with guns and other weapons on board *(n.)*
tons: a lot; more than 2,000 pounds *(n.)*
gathered: came together as a group; collected *(v.)*

3

| ready | warning | troops |
| outfox | communicate | attempting |

Date: _____

outfox: think around; cleverly trick *(v.)*
communicate: to share or give information *(v.)*
English Channel: a wide waterway between the island of England and France *(n.)*
choppy: rough; with lots of waves *(adj.)*
troops: soldiers *(n.)*

4

anchors	panicked	cannons
Calais	scrambling	rapidly
reorganize	swarmed	strategy
gunpowder	outmaneuver	

Date: _____

anchors: hooked metal weights used to hold boats still in water *(n.)*
gunpowder: a mixture of chemicals that produces explosive force *(n.)*
swarmed: covered; crawled over; crowded *(v.)*
outmaneuver: move quicker, faster, and more skillfully *(v.)*
strategy: a plan, usually for war or battle *(n.)*

5

| steered | mercy | pounded |
| shifted | | |

Date: _____

steered: controlled the direction of; guided *(v.)*
shifted: changed or moved *(v.)*
North Sea: a large body of water that is part of the Atlantic Ocean, located north of England *(n.)*

Mark this Flight on your timeline:

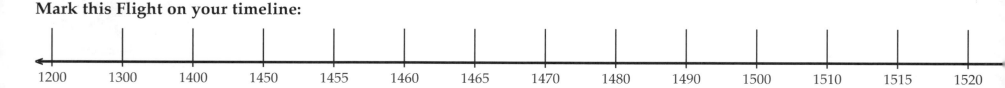

1200   1300   1400   1450   1455   1460   1465   1470   1480   1490   1500   1510   1515   1520

Post-Flight Debriefing

Use your imagery to answer questions for the whole Flight:

A. How would you summarize this Flight?

_____

_____

_____

B. Which of these is NOT true about the Spanish Armada?

    a) It included 130 ships when it set sail to invade England in 1588.
    b) The ships of the Spanish Armada were large and heavy.
    c) The Spanish ships outmaneuvered the English ships during the war.
    d) The Spanish cut their ships' anchors, leaving them at the mercy of the winds.

C. What did Drake do that kept the Spanish from invading for a year?

    a) He stole all their money so they couldn't afford enough ships.
    b) He filled their harbors with sand so they couldn't sail.
    c) He carried out a sneak attack, sinking the ships in their own harbor.
    d) none of the above

D. Why do you think the Spanish Armada failed to defeat England?

_____

_____

_____

The night sky lit up with flames. Drake's ship was close to the lead Armada ship. Then Drake and his sailors...

_____

_____

_____

_____

_____

_____

_____

_____

_____

_____

_____

_____

_____

_____

_____

_____

_____

530   1535   1540   1545   1550   1555   1565   1575   1585   1600   1700   1800   1900   2000

Flight 29

Pre-Flight for Mary, Queen of Scots

Preread words for each paragraph: **Study and visualize the vocabulary:**

1

Stuart	Scotland	power-hungry
Scottish	ensure	first-class
Guise	safety	

Date: _____

safety: protection from harm *(n.)*
power-hungry: wanting to control others *(adj.)*
first-class: the best; the most expensive *(adj.)*
ensure: make sure; make certain *(v.)*

2

obvious	impulsive	unsure
emotional	nervous	

Date: _____

obvious: clear; easy to understand *(adj.)*
impulsive: acting on sudden urges; acting without thinking *(adj.)*
conflict: a disagreement, fight, or difference *(n.)*
nervous: worried; overly scared; easily upset *(adj.)*
complained: whined or grumbled; expressed unhappiness with something *(v.)*

3

Darnley	kingly	dragged
planned	resented	begged
someday	secretary	horrified
realized	Rizzio	

Date: _____

kingly: like a ruler; regal *(adj.)*
resented: felt anger at or toward; felt hurt by *(v.)*
secretary: a person who writes down important information and handles duties *(n.)*
horrified: terrified; made sick with fear; shocked *(adj.)*

4

plotted	explosion	acquitted
seize	shook	proposed
settle	nobleman	infant
Kirk o'Field	Hepburn	abdicated

Date: _____

seize: to take by force *(v.)*
explosion: a blowing apart by force, usually related to a bomb *(n.)*
accused: blamed for wrongdoing *(v.)*
acquitted: cleared of wrongdoing by a court; found innocent *(v.)*
abdicated: gave up the claim to the throne or rulership of a country *(v.)*

5

protection	prison	convicted

Date: _____

prison: a place where criminals are held by force *(n.)*
overthrow: to remove from power *(v.)*
convicted: found guilty of wrongdoing by a court *(v.)*
protection: safety from harm *(n.)*

Mark this Flight on your timeline:

| 1200 | 1300 | 1400 | 1450 | 1455 | 1460 | 1465 | 1470 | 1480 | 1490 | 1500 | 1510 | 1515 | 1520 |

Post-Flight Debriefing

Use your imagery to answer questions for the whole Flight:

A. What is the main idea for this Flight?

_____

_____

_____

B. Which of these did NOT happen to Mary, Queen of Scots?

a) She witnessed her husband killing her dear friend David Rizzio.
b) She had the Queen of England beheaded, and took the throne for herself.
c) She spent 19 years under guard.
d) She was married three times.

C. Whom did Mary give the throne to?

a) her husband, Lord Darnley
b) her cousin, Elizabeth
c) her infant son, James
d) her grown son, David

D. Why did Elizabeth have Mary executed?

_____

_____

_____

Write a Word Summary for all that you have learned about Mary, Queen of Scots.

_____

_____

_____

_____

_____

_____

_____

_____

_____

_____

_____

_____

_____

| 530 | 1535 | 1540 | 1545 | 1550 | 1555 | 1565 | 1575 | 1585 | 1600 | 1700 | 1800 | 1900 | 2000 |

Pre-Flight for Elizabethan Age

Preread words for each paragraph:

Study and visualize the vocabulary:

1

monarchs   dominate   Elizabethan
flourished

Date: _____

monarchs: rulers; kings or queens *(n.)*
dominate: to overpower; to have influence over *(v.)*
cub: the baby or the young of some wild animal *(n.)*

2

sponsored   Shakespeare   hawk
troupes   physically   watching
traveling   riding   matches
perform

Date: _____

dabbling: doing a bit of; trying *(v.)*
sponsored: paid for *(v.)*
troupes: groups of actors or entertainers *(n.)*
physically: in or of the body *(adj.)*
tennis: a game where a ball is bounced over a net with racquets *(n.)*

3

average   salt-preserved   audience
expanding   spoil   veils
cinnamon   role

Date: _____

expanding: getting bigger *(v.)*
cinnamon: a brown spice from Asia that tastes sweet and bitter *(n.)*
salt-preserved: packed in salt to stop decay *(adj.)*
spoil: to go bad or rot *(v.)*
veils: cloths worn to cover the face and/or head *(n.)*

4

peaceful   prosperous   wilderness

Date: _____

globe: the whole world; a sphere with a map of the world on it *(n.)*
imported: brought in from elsewhere *(v.)*
prosperous: doing well *(adj.)*

5

fair   overcrowding   prosper
diplomat   era

Date: _____

diplomat: a person who helps maintain a country's affairs with other countries *(n.)*
overcrowding: too many people moving into a small area *(n.)*
era: a time period *(n.)*
prosper: to do well *(v.)*

Mark this Flight on your timeline:

| 1200 | 1300 | 1400 | 1450 | 1455 | 1460 | 1465 | 1470 | 1480 | 1490 | 1500 | 1510 | 1515 | 1520 |

Post-Flight Debriefing

Use your imagery to answer questions for the whole Flight:

A. What is this Flight about?

_____

_____

_____

B. How long did Elizabeth rule England?

    a) 10 years
    b) 39 days
    c) 45 years
    d) 25 years

C. Which major change occurred during the Elizabethan Age?

    a) The population of England grew because a cure for the plague
       had been found.
    b) Expanding trade brought goods and spices into the average home.
    c) Women were now allowed to have parts in plays.
    d) all of the above

D. What is a good picture for life during the Elizabethan Age?

_____

_____

Write a Picture Summary for this Flight.

_____

_____

_____

_____

_____

_____

_____

_____

_____

_____

_____

_____

1530   1535   1540   1545   1550   1555   1565   1575   1585   1600   1700   1800   1900   2000

Flight 31

Pre-Flight for Shakespeare

Preread words for each paragraph:

Study and visualize the vocabulary:

1

Date: _____

William	Hathaway	actor
Stratford	Hamnet	playwright
upon	Judith	critics
Avon	mystery	criticized

mystery: a type of story that leaves one in suspense until the end *(n.)*
actor: a person who pretends to be other people for plays *(n.)*
playwright: a person who writes entertainment for the stage, known as plays *(n.)*
critics: people who review and write about art *(n.)*

2

Date: _____

swept   Chamberlain's   eighteen
closed

swept: moved quickly *(v.)*
investing: putting money or time into *(v.)*
closed: made to shut down *(v.)*

3

Date: _____

recent	strictly	Olivia
somewhat	factual	rejects
notorious	comedies	Cesario
villains	identity	Viola
assumed	Duke Orsino	disguise

notorious: famous or well known for being bad *(adj.)*
side-splitting: funny; causing enough laughter to make the stomach hurt *(adj.)*
woo: to seek to marry; to pay romantic attention *(v.)*
posing: pretending; to be standing or sitting in a certain way *(v.)*
disguise: clothing, wigs, and other elements used to hide one's appearance *(n.)*

4

Date: _____

Romeo	masquerade	potion
Juliet	tragedy	grieving
feuding	banished	entwined

feuding: fighting *(v.)*
masquerade: a type of party where costumes or masks are worn *(n.)*
ball: a grand party, usually with dancing *(n.)*
tragedy: a drama in which characters suffer; a sad event or disaster *(n.)*
banished: sent away from *(v.)*

5

Date: _____

Cleopatra	themes	flawed
Lear	comic	

retired: stopped working *(v.)*
comic: funny; causing laughter and amusement *(adj.)*
movies: motion pictures, films, or features *(n.)*
themes: central ideas or main patterns in a story *(n.)*
regarded: considered; thought of *(v.)*

Mark this Flight on your timeline:

← | 1200 | 1300 | 1400 | 1450 | 1455 | 1460 | 1465 | 1470 | 1480 | 1490 | 1500 | 1510 | 1515 | 1520

Post-Flight Debriefing

Use your imagery to answer questions for the whole Flight:

A. What is this Flight about?

_____

_____

B. What did Shakespeare do for a living?

    a) He wrote plays.
    b) He managed a theater.
    c) He was an actor.
    d) all of the above

C. Which of these is NOT the style of one of Shakespeare's plays?

    a) history
    b) comedy
    c) horror
    d) tragedy

D. Why do you think Shakespeare's plays are still read and performed today?

_____

_____

Describe what you visualized for one of Shakespeare's plays.

_____

_____

_____

_____

_____

_____

_____

_____

_____

_____

_____

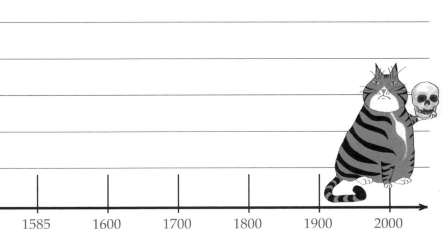

| 530 | 1535 | 1540 | 1545 | 1550 | 1555 | 1565 | 1575 | 1585 | 1600 | 1700 | 1800 | 1900 | 2000 |

Flight 32

Pre-Flight for Cervantes

Preread words for each paragraph:

Study and visualize the vocabulary:

1

Miguel
Cervantes

Alcalá
Madrid

sidetracked
debt

settled: made a home in *(v.)*
sidetracked: distracted *(v.)*
joined: enrolled or signed up with *(v.)*
release: a freeing from confinement *(n.)*
debt: an amount of money owed *(n.)*

Date: _____

2

tax
decent
Don
Quixote
suit

countryside
justice
squire
Sancho

Panza
voice
reality

tax collector: a person whose job it is to collect or get taxes *(n.)*
decent: moral; proper or correct; good enough *(adj.)*
justice: the law carried out fairly *(n.)*
fantasies: daydreams; pictures from the imagination *(n.)*
squire: a servant to a knight *(n.)*

Date: _____

3

knighthood

chivalry

vanes

chivalry: the rules of behavior for knights; brave actions *(n.)*
breeze: a light wind *(n.)*
points out: aims a finger at; calls attention to *(v.)*
vanes: long blades attached to a windmill that turn in the wind *(n.)*
exclaims: says loudly; shouts *(v.)*

Date: _____

4

stallion
renames
Dulcinea

Toboso
Mambrino

situations
tongue

stallion: a male horse *(n.)*
deeds: actions *(n.)*
herds: groups *(n.)*
situations: the way things are at given moments; circumstances *(n.)*

Date: _____

5

fortune

widely

fortune: money; wealth *(n.)*
widely: over a large area *(adv.)*

Date: _____

Mark this Flight on your timeline:

| 1200 | 1300 | 1400 | 1450 | 1455 | 1460 | 1465 | 1470 | 1480 | 1490 | 1500 | 1510 | 1515 | 1520 |

Post-Flight Debriefing

Date: _____

Use your imagery to answer questions for the whole Flight:

A. How would you summarize this Flight?

_____

_____

_____

B. Which of these did NOT happen to Cervantes during his life?

a) He joined the Spanish Army.
b) He was left on a deserted island for 15 years.
c) He spent time in prison.
d) He was held captive by pirates.

C. What is Cervantes' book *Don Quixote* about?

a) an explorer who discovers the New World
b) an old man living in a fantasy world who goes on adventures
c) a brave young knight who fights in many battles
d) a young prince who falls in love with a peasant girl

D. Why do you think *Don Quixote* remains one of the most loved books ever written?

_____

_____

_____

Don Quixote saw the barber holding a bowl of water that was actually the magical Helmet of Mambrino. Determined to win the helmet, he...

_____

_____

_____

_____

_____

_____

_____

_____

_____

_____

_____

_____

1530   1535   1540   1545   1550   1555   1565   1575   1585   1600   1700   1800   1900   2000

Flight 33

Pre-Flight for Galileo

Preread words for each paragraph: **Study and visualize the vocabulary:**

1

Galileo	remembered	Pisa	
Galilei	solar	intensely	
founder			

founder: a creator; the person who starts something *(n.)*

solar system: the sun and the planets that move around it *(n.)*

intensely: very strongly *(adv.)*

Date: _____

2

geometry	argue	heartbeat
beliefs	loudly	pendulum

geometry: a type of math that studies angles, lines, shapes, etc. *(n.)*

content: satisfied or happy *(adj.)*

swinging: moving from side to side *(v.)*

pendulum: a heavy weight that hangs from a fixed point and swings back and forth a regular motion *(n.)*

Date: _____

3

gravity	according	weights

gravity: a force that pulls objects to the ground *(n.)*

weights: heavy objects, usually made of metal *(n.)*

speed: the rate at which something moves *(n.)*

proving: finding out if something is true or not *(v.)*

force: the amount of push or pull *(n.)*

Date: _____

4

optician	observe	Jupiter
magnify		

optician: a person who makes and repairs eyeglasses *(n.)*

lens: a piece of curved glass designed to form images *(n.)*

magnify: to make something look bigger *(v.)*

sun spots: black spots on the sun *(n.)*

findings: results or discoveries *(n.)*

Date: _____

5

illegal	proven	confined

declared: stated or said *(v.)*

illegal: against the law *(adj.)*

cell: a small room *(n.)*

sentenced: given a punishment by a court *(v.)*

house arrest: the state of being kept in a house against one's will *(n.)*

Date: _____

Mark this Flight on your timeline:

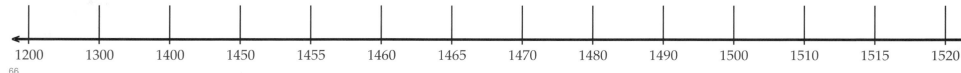

1200 1300 1400 1450 1455 1460 1465 1470 1480 1490 1500 1510 1515 1520

Post-Flight Debriefing

Use your imagery to answer questions for the whole Flight:

A. What is the main concept for this Flight?

_____

_____

_____

B. What did Galileo want to study instead of medicine?

    a) history
    b) the law
    c) math
    d) philosophy

C. What did Galileo invent to help him see the stars and planets better?

    a) the space shuttle
    b) the telescope
    c) the digital camera
    d) the airplane

D. Why do you think Galileo is an important figure of history?

_____

_____

_____

Write a Picture Summary for all your imagery for this Flight.

_____

_____

_____

_____

_____

_____

_____

_____

_____

_____

_____

_____

1530   1535   1540   1545   1550   1555   1565   1575   1585   1600   1700   1800   1900   2000